hand felted jewelry and beads

hand felted jewelry and beads

25 ARTFUL DESIGNS

Carol Huber Cypher

INTERWEAVE PRESS
www.interweave.com

Art Director: Paulette Livers
Design: Karen Schober
Photography: Joe Coca
Illustration: Gayle Ford

Interweave Press LLC
201 East Fourth Street
Loveland, CO 80537
www.interweave.com

Printed in China through Asia Pacific Offset.

Library of Congress Cataloging-in-Publication Data
Cypher, Carol Huber.
  Hand felted jewelry and beads : 25 artful designs / Carol Huber Cypher.
     p. cm.
  Includes index.
  ISBN-13: 978-1-59668-005-0
  ISBN-10: 1-59668-005-9
 1. Felt work. 2. Jewelry making. 3. Beadwork. I. Title.
  TT849.5.H36 2006
  745.594'2--dc22
                          2005027195

10 9 8 7 6 5 4 3 2

acknowledgments

●●●

Morton Jay Cypher, "Morty" to his dear friends, my true love and husband for twenty-six years, tolerates, even encourages, my doing whatever I need to do in my creative career: appropriate the kitchen for more studio space during a felting frenzy, work all night long, felt my hair into locks, abandon a secure career with benefits and pension to pursue a tenuous livelihood of beadwork/feltmaking. Foreseeing my need, he has outfitted me with the requisite electronic accoutrements of a twenty-first century artist/author/teacher. He didn't grouse about my share of domestic things that went neglected in deference to my writing. He remains my friend, confidant, lover, critic, and voice of reason.

Thank you, Dad, for instilling in me the quiet confidence that I can do anything.

Amy Raff has helped me navigate the e-waves sufficiently to execute this book. I am very grateful for her sage counsel and lifelong friendship. Cherished friend, Susan Vazquez is a font of fiber knowledge. Her teaching me to spin, selling me a wheel, and inviting me to join her "loosely twisted group of spinners," fueled this passion for fiber that has become my career. Susan introduced me to Phyllis Dintenfass, fellow bead aficionado and trusted sounding board. I rely on Phyllis's informed, intelligent, and insightful perspective.

I enjoy volleying words about with wordmeister and purveyor of fine wool, Radley Cramer.

Deep appreciation to the students and fiber artists willing to part with their work for a few months for sharing in the gallery here.

Thank you, Betsy Armstrong, Acquiring Editor at Interweave Press for giving my book wings.

Thanks to my Editor, Christine Townsend, for her enthusiasm, bright spirit, and capable guidance into this process; and Managing Editor, Rebecca Campbell, for cheerfully, professionally, and confidently seeing this project through. Technical Editor Jean Lampe, I love your laughter, admire your thoroughness, and appreciate your help.

contents

PART ONE

The Process

Introduction

• • •

Felt is organic and humble and primal, yet ethereal and beautiful and sensuous. It is warm and soft and yielding, yet strong and hard and dense. No animal dies in its making. As a medium of adornment, felt combines the sensuality of fine fiber with the shapely qualities of sculpture. Over several years of teaching feltmaking workshops I remain captivated by the magical qualities of the medium, the sense of wonder that it instills in the novice, and the endless inspiration it offers the seasoned pro.

Feltmaking comprises two processes: felting and fulling. *Felting* is the tangling of the fibers, (accomplished by either wet **or** dry methods); *fulling* shrinks and hardens the felt by steaming, beating, rolling or needling.

Some elbow grease is required, but the small scale of the pieces in this book prevents the work from being exhausting.

Felt, the earliest of textiles, is strong, resilient, and versatile. Wool fiber is covered with overlapping scales called cuticle (think roof shingles). In traditional feltmaking, fibers are pressed together, mingled and agitated in the presence of hot water (which opens and lifts the scales/cuticle). Then, in the process of closing, the scales snag neighboring fibers, creating felt. (Think Velcro). Continued agitation, steam-

ing or beating further compacts and condenses the felt (the second stage of feltmaking called fulling).

A BRIEF HISTORY OF FELT

Felt has been used for housing, rugs, bags, carriers, clothing, bedding, furnishings, and decorative items. Intact items from the Bronze and Iron Ages have been unearthed from frozen burial grounds in the Altai mountains, the range shared by Kazakhstan, Russia, Mongolia, and China. Discoveries include saddle blankets, wall hangings, and tapestries.

Generations of nomads of central Asia have lived in round tents, known as yurts or *gers*, made of felt panels on collapsible wooden frames. The thick wool panels provide protection from wind, rain, and snow and on warm days can be rolled up. During precipita-

tion, the property of horizontal felt (roof) to hold water but vertical felt (walls) to shed it is an advantage. Nomadic furniture and flooring is also made of felt, providing a home and contents that can be dissembled and reassembled elsewhere in just a couple of hours.

The *kepenek*, a shepherd's thick felt cocoon, is still used today as cloak, sleeping bag, and lean-to shelter from the windy steppes.

TRADITIONAL FELTMAKING

Historically, producing a felt panel or rug required several workers and an animal. The wool locks had to be teased into tufts of lofty fluff, then piled in layers on top of a mat of "mother felt" (the worn felt that would be retired when the new one was produced). Intricate designs of rich colors were laid in the final layer. The wool was dampened and rolled up tight and tied, then pulled behind an animal until the pressure and agitation made the fibers felt. The more agitation and pressure, the thicker, stronger, and denser the felt became.

This very same technique is employed worldwide today. Contemporary feltmakers may use reed, rush, cane mats, or even bubble wrap in place of mother felt to lay out and roll up their wool, but the process remains the same. Felting machines and their mechanized rolling or vibrating may relieve the feltmaker of labor, but they are not able to improve on this age-old craft.

needle felting

Today felt composed of blends that contain little or no wool is made industrially by the dry technique of needle felting.

Opposing beds of thousands of felt needles move toward and then away from each other while fibers are introduced between them. Tiny barbs on the needles make the fibers in their path knot and tangle. Repeated pushes with the needles create more knots and tangles closer together. 100 percent synthetic felt is produced this way.

Unlike traditional wet feltmaking, which relies on the structure of individual fibers, dry needle felting tangles entire fibers irrespective of their structure. Any fiber can be felted by dry needle felting. Wool-blends and synthetic felts for road pavement subsurfaces, "pleather" for sneakers, and acrylic felt yardage are produced this way.

Felt needles come in various gauges with varying barb placement. Most are three-sided, a triangle as seen from the point, with barbs on the edges. Star-shaped needles offer more surfaces.

Traditional feltmakers use needles to incorporate fine details into their work before wet-felting. Once a wet-felted piece is dry, needle-felting may produce more surface design, as well as shaping. Some feltmakers work exclusively in dry needle-felting technique, creating both flat pieces and sculpture of finesse and remarkable detail.

HOW TO USE THIS BOOK

This is a handbook of compact felt-making; that is, projects in a scale that is accessible to everyone, everywhere. Collectively, the projects provide a comprehensive feltmaking curriculum, covering every aspect of the craft: flat, flat with a resist, felting on a form, creating three-dimensional felt, all using wet or traditional feltmaking. The book also covers dry or needle felting plus the combination of wet and dry felting.

The skills acquired through making these projects are basic to all feltmaking. With more space, tools, and supplies, these skills can easily produce yardage, hats, mittens, slippers, boots, tea cozies, vessels, wall hangings, rugs, purses, totes, window treatments, table runners, blankets and all the felted items you can imagine.

Instructions for the projects in this book are written as recipes. It assumes that the work will take place in an Essential Feltmaker's Studio (a space at the counter or table plus the few supplies listed on pages 5 through 18) using the quantity of the ingredients listed. Detailed step-by-step instruction refers to technique basics (pages 19 through 23) that may include "pull wisps," "layer the wool," "flat felting," "felt a rope," "towel dry" . . .

So select a project and follow the recipe. The accumulation of projects will build and refine your feltmaking and beadwork skills, but there is no particular order to follow, and no experience required.

Use this book to find your own wooly voice to express your inner feltiness.

CHAPTER 1

The Essential Feltmaker's Studio (The Tools)

• • • •

It is easy to create a feltmaking studio for every project in this book. Assemble these few ordinary items—your feltmaking tools—in a basket or box. Your felt-maker's studio is that container plus a tray table or countertop.

LIST OF TOOLS

Bubble wrap
Plastic
Roller
Tie
Hot, soapy water
Skewer
Foam
Felt needle
Towels
Friction cloth
Scissors
Blade
Size 18 tapestry needle
Doll needle
Size 10 beading needle
Crimp tool

ABOUT THE TOOLS

bubble wrap, 18 x 24" (45.5 × 61 cm)

You don't have to use bubble wrap, any flexible textured surface to roll your work in and on will do. A sushi mat will serve for small pieces; a bamboo placemat from an import store is an ideal size for most pieces here. Any rush, reed, or cane beach mat or window blind is suitable. I once successfully used a ridged rubber doormat, but I prefer bubble wrap. The bubble wrap used for packing material is adequate. Swimming-pool solar covers are huge sheets of heavyweight bubble wrap. I purchase them from pool supply stores and cut them to size for workshops, kits, and my own use.

Note: Recipes make a distinction of bubble-side up or bubble-side down. If the wool is layered on the bubble-side up, when water is added, some wool will sink into the crevices between the bubbles and alter the design of the wool. Hence we arrange the wool on the smooth side up. When we seek texture to roll the wool against when, say making rope, we use the bubble side up.

plastic

Any plastic sheet will work but, the crinkly, noisy high-density plastic works best.

roller

Foam pipe insulation from the hard-ware store is cheap and wonderful. You can custom-size it with any

HOW TO TIE UP FELTWORK

A gallery assistant and student of mine at Brookfield Craft Center shared the way feltmaker Beth Beede taught her to tie up feltwork. Wrap the stocking tie around the rolled-up work and tie once, pulling tight enough to make a waist in the roll. Then, without letting go of the tie, swap hands and pull. If your left hand pulled the tie end away and the right hand pulled the other tie end towards you, simply swap the direction you pull: pull the left hand toward you and the right hand away. Doing so usually holds the roll together until it is time to unroll and reroll.

scissors large enough to fit around it or a serrated (bread) knife.

tie

Retired pantyhose are ideal. Cut the feet off, then cut across the legs every three or four inches to produce several bands of nylon. Cut each band once to create a tie whose stretchiness and strength is ideal for securing rolled-up work during the fulling process. Tie in a bow or as described in sidebar on page 5.

cup or bowl of hot, soapy water

A couple of drops of soap—glycerine, castile, dish, or Murphy's Oil—stirred into a cup of water. For traveling, I pack a bar of glycerine soap to avoid the disaster of spills.

skewer

Choose bamboo or wood for their grainy surface; don't use metal.

foam

Choose an inexpensive dishwashing sponge or piece of cushion foam. Avoid cellulose sponges because they retain too much moisture and rust felt needles. Keeping foam (or a sponge) behind the wool you are needle-felting is a clean and painless alternative to using your thigh or palm. Poking yourself with the felt needle *really* hurts, plus you don't want to get blood in the work. Once the felt becomes dense, you may

Ties

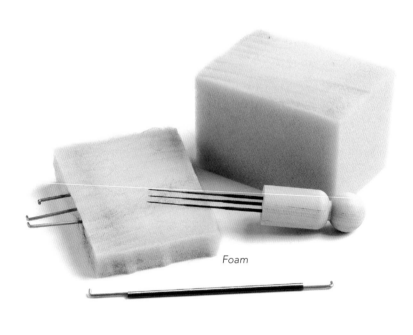

Foam

These items are: (clockwise from bottom left) friction cloth, bubble wrap, foam roller, towel, foam sponge, plastic.

enjoy working without the sponge or foam.

felt needle

They are usually about a dollar, so live it up and collect many styles in gauges 36 to 40. There are innumerable configurations of barbs. Some needles have eight barbs on one of three edges. Others have three barbs on each edge. The barbs on some are within a half-inch of the tip while the barbs on others are placed every half inch along the edge. And the star-shaped needles offer more than three edges with their assortment of barb placements.

There are holders that combine three or more needles. The small ones that cluster three needles are wonderful but, use a single needle for decorating.

towels

Have one or two available every time you work. Always handle dry wool with dry hands. Wipe up spills. A damp towel beneath rolled-up work prevents it from slipping.

friction cloth

Cut a 24 × 18" (61 × 45.5 cm) piece of this rubbery shelf lining/carpet under-liner sold in rolls at hardware stores. It prevents things placed on it from sliding, and it's handy in the feltmaker's studio.

scissors

It is amazing how quickly such a soft and gentle fiber as wool can dull a pair of scissors. Dedicate a pair of

CRIMP TOOL

Specialty pliers designed to secure clasps to jewelry by crimping small metal beads over doubled beading wire. This tool will help you produce consistent, professional, and enduring crimping. The regular-sized pliers will work beautifully with medium beading wire. Two additional sizes, micro and maximized, accommodate thin-gauge and heavy-gauge wires. Inspect the tool while squeezing it shut. Notice that there are two openings. The inside one resembles the silhouette of lips, the outer one the silhouette of an eye.

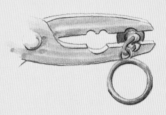

To use: Place a crimp bead on the wire, an optional seed bead or two, and your clasp (by passing the wire through the loop on the clasp). Run the beading wire back through the seed bead(s) and the crimp bead. Open the crimp tool. Allow the crimp bead to lie in the lower lip and adjust the two beading wires to lie parallel within the crimp bead. Squeeze the crimp tool. The hanging-down center of the upper lip depresses or crimps the crimp bead to secure the wires. Loosen your grip and slide the crimp bead into the outer chamber, end to end. Squeeze the pliers to fold the crimp bead in half; this minimized appearance produces professional beadwork.

inexpensive yet sharp ones for felting. There is a handy little tool in the sewing aisle of craft stores to hone the scissor edge. Pick one up. Fiskars makes a small key chain version and a 4 × 4" (10 × 10 cm) tabletop model.

blade

A package of single-edged razor blades is useful for incising felt. I also keep a thin-bladed, cheap cook's knife that I can sharpen with a pass or two through a sharpener.

size 18 tapestry needle

Useful for stringing small felt beads on beading wire or other stringing material.

size 10 beading needle

If you quilt or sew, you may be comfortable with short sharps needles. I prefer the longer bead needle. Size 10 will suit most of your needs. It is the beefiest and largest-eye needle that will fit through most beads. If you are inclined to work with very tiny seed beads, size 15° or smaller, choose a size 13 needle.

doll needle

These needles are 4 to 8" (10 to 20.5 cm) long and are useful for passing through long areas of felt with thread, beading wire, or other stringing material.

Silk ribbon, silk rattail cord, doll needle, and size 18 tapestry needle

CHAPTER 2

The Ingredients

• • •

WOOL

Wool is protein (keratin) fiber that is shorn from sheep. It is categorized by characteristics such as length, crimp, micron size/Bradford count, softness, and luster. Soft and elastic wool, such as Cormo, is comfortable next to the skin and is appropriate for woven, knitted, or felted clothing. Conversely, the long coarse fiber of Lincoln sheep, unsuitable for clothing, makes a durable rug capable of rich color and high luster. Characteristics vary among sheep breeds, sometimes within the breed, and, as in the case of Icelandic sheep, even among single-breed fleeces.

Breeds vary in their capacity to felt and in the quality of the felt they produce. Merino and Rambouillet create a fine felt whose smooth finish is ideal for wearing next to the skin. These fibers are luxurious to handle and work with. Their low luster is the perfect foil to glass embellishments.

batts versus roving

Processed wool is available as carded batts and carded or combed roving (a thick rope of fiber). Carded fibers, though aligned, are relatively random compared to combed, whose fibers are all arranged parallel. Both forms felt readily. It can be argued that carded batts are the more efficient choice because they require less care in how each layer of fiber is oriented, but the painterly capacity of combed fiber to produce color nuances that resemble brushstrokes,

Wool

ALTERNATIVE FIBERS

Soy Silk is a wonderful new fiber that rivals the shine and feel of silk. Vegans are relieved to know that no silkworms are sacrificed in its production. Although it's derived from plants, Soy Silk is a protein fiber, a byproduct of tofu production that shares more properties with silk and wool than with other plant-derived fibers.

Roving

makes it my choice hands down. Combed roving, also called sliver (pronounced with a long ī) is readily available in a vast array of delicious solid colors and blends (see Resources, page 119). Avoid accidentally purchasing "superwash" fiber that has been treated to prevent the cuticle from opening. Spinners spin this to produce a wool yarn that cannot be carelessly felted, shrunken, or fulled.

how to handle wool

Grasp the tip of one end of the roving with one hand. Place your other hand around the roving about 8" (20.5 cm) away from the end. Pull gently. The fibers in your grasp drift away from the roving in wisps of parallel fibers. Notice the length of the fibers (staple length). Attempting to pull fiber out of the roving with your hands held less than the staple length apart is a struggle that tears the fibers. Simply allow the distance between your hands to exceed the staple length when you pull off wisps of fiber.

wool choice for needle felting

My wool of choice for needle felting is Romney. Its coarseness

and medium crimp (a word that describes the fiber's waviness) make it easy to work with the needle. Merino wool is too fine and permits nothing but the finest gauge felt needle to penetrate—and even they leave pockmarks. That said, I often use Merino wool for surface design.

SYNTHETIC FIBERS

Because the needle felting process does not rely on the cuticle of the fiber, it does not require wool fiber. Polyester batting used for pillow stuffing works well. Needle felted projects can be made entirely free of wool. Metallic fibers and synthetic fibers such as Mylar and flash work for surface design, and for blending with wool or polyester.

SILK AND THE NEW NATURAL FIBERS

Silk and the new natural fibers such as corn silk (ingeo) and Soy Silk add luster and rich color to felt.

Synthetic fibers, top; bombyx silk, center; Soy Silk, bottom

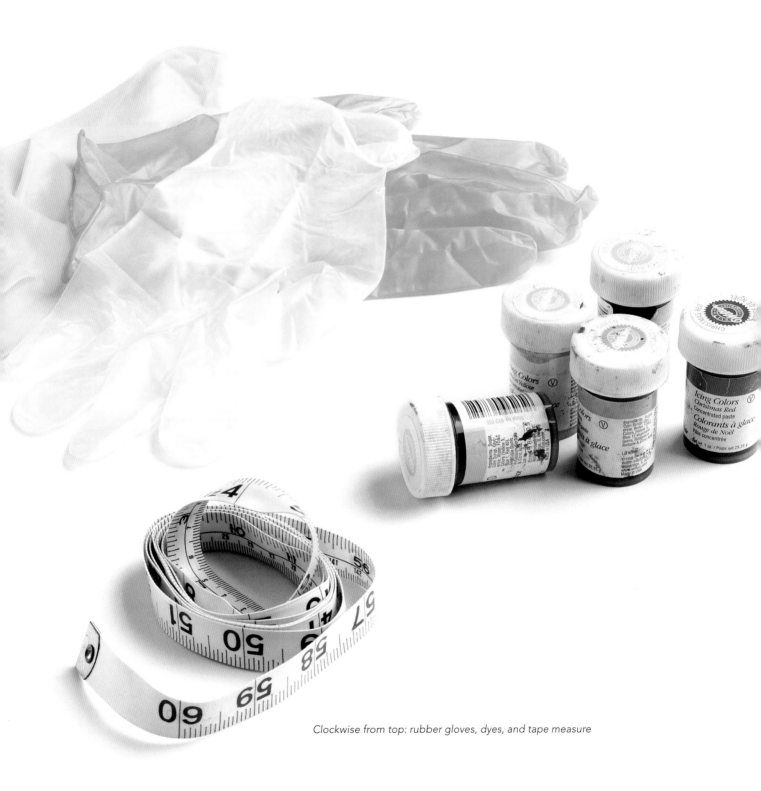

Clockwise from top: rubber gloves, dyes, and tape measure

These fibers, alone or carded with other fibers, can be needled into the felt with felt needles or used as surface design by wet-felting a thin layer into the wool.

DYEING WOOL AND OTHER PROTEIN FIBERS

My brief foray into dyeing involved a reed basket with purple cotton handles that I decided to dye forest green. Although I selected the appropriate dye and followed the directions to the letter, the outcome was a teal basket with cobalt blue handles. Sweet mystery. And when I told my basketmaking, fiber enthusiast friends about my adventure, no one shed light on the mysterious color change, but many made alarmist remarks about its potential for poisoning.

Desperate for color and intimidated by the scope and toxicity of dyeing, I use a safe and kitchen-friendly, albeit still unpredictable, method of coloring protein fibers; icing dye! It comes in little jars redolent of finger paints, and you can find it in the confectionary/bakery supply aisles of craft stores and in some supermarkets. Approach it with a spirit of adventure and fun. But wear gloves!

With so many beautiful fibers commercially available, it's unnecessary to dye your own. But, if you have light-colored natural wool, silk, soy or other protein fiber and need a palette of colored wool, here is an easy and safe method I use.

RECIPE FOR DYEING PROTEIN FIBERS (WOOL, SILK, SOY SILK)

have on hand
Microwave oven
Freezer paper or vinyl covering for table
Plastic food-wrap film
Microwave-safe casserole dish or bowl
Spoon
Paintbrush
Disposable gloves

ingredients
Wool, silk, or Soy Silk fiber, yarn, or fabric
Jars of icing dye in a variety of colors
White vinegar
Water

Space-dyed/hand-painted fiber provides an array of color at once. Protect the work table with freezer paper or vinyl. Lay down the plastic food-wrap film.

In the casserole dish or bowl, mix one part white vinegar with three parts room-temperature water. Dunk the fiber and then hold it over the bowl for a moment to allow it to drain. Lay out the fiber on the plastic film. Paint the fiber with the icing dye using your gloved fingers or paintbrushes. Leave space between the colors so they can bleed into each other. Fold the edges of the plastic film over the fiber.

Fold the fiber into a bundle that will fit inside the microwave oven. Nuke for 4 minutes at full power. Allow the fiber to cool completely to room temperature.

Rinse the fiber (wear gloves) in room-temperature water. *Note*: If you rush this process and rinse the fiber before it is cool, it seems that all the colors discharge to fuchsia. Unless you really love fuchsia, allow the fiber to cool.

Another warning: If you rinse wool fiber vigorously or in hot water, it will felt.

Hang the fiber to dry.

Dyed wool

Chapter 3

Beading on Felt

• • •

Beading and felting are similar in many ways: intense and engaging process, composed of tiny units, wide range of color, impact that is both visual and tactile, and prized throughout history as talismanic and magical.

However, it is their contrast that makes their combination so provocative, enhancing and under-scoring the qualities of each. The reflective properties and sharp definition of the brilliant, cool, dense, glass beads are magnified when paired with matte, warm, fuzzy, light-absorbing felt.

NEEDLE

I always use a beading needle, size 10, because I am much happier regarding the activity as beading instead of sewing. If I use beads size 15˚ or smaller, I use a size 13 needle. Feel free to use any needle that will pass through the beads you choose.

THREAD
type

Use any thread that fits into the eye of your needle and your beads. Cotton will not endure like polyester and nylon. I generally use nylon beading thread in size D, available in a vast array of colors, unless I expect to heat the felt by steaming or ironing, which shrinks and stiffens the thread. A good choice in this case is polyester or poly blend.

color

Base your choice of thread color on the predominant color of the work unless you're using transparent beads. When using transparent beads, consider the impact that the thread's color will have on the beads' appearance. A gray thread inside pastel transparent beads will give the appearance of washed-out color. Yellow thread will brighten the beads and alter the color. For example, transparent blue beads will appear green and transparent red beads will appear orange. Given a choice, select a slightly darker over a slightly lighter thread. Light colors jump out of the background, while dark colors recede.

When choices are few, go with the wisdom of generations of quilters who default to gray.

how much?

I always recommend using a wingspan of thread. Our wingspan approximates our height. Extend your arms out from your side, perpendicular to your body. If you work with your wingspan of thread folded nearly doubled but used singly, simply extending your arm will always pull the thread through.

If you insist on longer thread, you have to reel it in with each stitch or bead, giving it the opportunity to catch and tangle. Also, by the time you reel the thread in, you've forgotten what your next intention was.

Short thread is fine and many sewers are quite insistent that short thread is the measure of a fine and decidedly superior sewer.

anchor the thread to the felt

Pass the needle through the felt anywhere. Pull the tail into the felt. Pass the needle under a few fibers at the exit location and make a half hitch (before pulling the thread all the way through, pass the needle into the loop of thread and pull tight). Pass back through the exit

*Hank of Czech seed beads, tubes of Japanese seed beads,
threads, Japanese color-lined drops, needles*

point and make another half hitch where the needle exits. Be careful not to pull the thread so tight that the felt dimples.

At this point, follow the instructions included with the project and either pass the needle back into the felt for the next step or pass back into the felt a short distance, exit, then cut the thread close to the work. (If the thread is cut directly at the half hitch, it can easily slide open and leave a bit of thread to flap around and reduce the number of half hitches.)

SEWING ON BEADS

Embroider elaborate designs using all the following stitches and more. Relish the ease and versatility and joy of beading on felt. Thrill to the powerful combination of shiny glass beads on the matte background that felt provides.

Direct the needle to exit wherever you wish to place a bead. Pick up one or more beads. Let them drop down to the felt's surface. At the far end of the bead(s), sink the tip of the needle into the felt (lazy stitch) directed toward where you wish to place another bead.

BEAD DOTS

To dot the felt with a single bead, bring the needle out of the felt at the place where you want to add the bead. Pick up a bead. Drop the needle back into the felt only a bead's distance away.

STACKED BEADS/FRINGE

Pick up the stack of beads. Allow them to fall to the work, stacked on the thread. Pass back through all of them except the topmost, referred to as a turning bead. The turning bead allows you to pass back through the beads just added without them all falling off. This same principle applies to making fringe. The number of beads that are to dangle in the fringe are picked up on the needle. Then a turning bead(s) is/are selected. Then the needle is passed back through all the other beads.

HIDING KNOTS

One of the many wonderful things about beading on felt is that even very thin felt is thick enough to hide thread. So carry the thread through the felt and surface only where you wish to place more beads. It is not necessary or desirable that the thread show on the back or anywhere.

Occasionally make a half hitch as you work. That way, if the thread carrying the beads accidentally gets caught on something, the felt will not pucker and warp.

CREATE LINES OF BEADS
lazy stitch

Pick up 5 or so beads. Let them fall to the work and lie on the felt. Drop the needle down into the felt right at the end of the beads. Pass through the felt and come back out of the felt. Pick up 3 to 5 more beads and again enter the felt, surfacing to repeat for the entire length desired.

backstitch

Come out of the felt, pick up 5 or more beads, allow them to fall to the work, pass into the felt at the last bead, and exit from the felt 2 beads back and pass through the last 2 beads again. Go on to add 3, 4, or more beads and again enter the felt and exit from the felt to pass through the last bead or 2 again.

couching

Bead a surface design using a strand of beads. Lay the strand on the felt. Bring an anchored thread up over the thread of the strand and drop the needle back into the felt. Surface the needle a few beads' distance away and again tack down the carrying thread of the strand. Anchor both ends of the carrying thread into the felt.

BEADED EDGINGS
whipstitch

Add beads to each whipstitch along an edge. Bring the needle out of the felt ¼ to ½" (6 mm to 1.3 cm) in from the edge. Pick up 5 to 7 beads. Bring the needle around the edge and come up through the felt, from the back to the front, a bead's distance from where the thread came out.

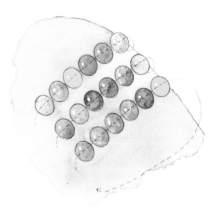

blanket stitch

Pick up 3, 5, or 7 beads right near the edge. Allow them to lie along the edge. Pass the needle into the felt right there. Bring the needle back around and up under the thread. Doing so situates the beads along the edge. Repeat as desired along the edge.

picot

Near the edge of the felt, pick up 3 beads. Pass the needle through the very edge of the felt, only a bead's distance away. Pass the needle back up the last bead.

From now on, pick up only 2 beads. Pass the needle through the very edge of the felt, only a bead's distance away. Pass the needle back up the last bead.

TURNING BEADS

A turning bead is not simply a device to keep the fringe or stacked beads from falling off. When you are stacking beads, make the turning bead a tinier one to display the stack to its full advantage. When you are creating fringe—beaded stamens are but one example—use a special bead for the turning bead. This could be a pearl, gemstone, drop bead, or crystal. Or consider using 3 or 5 beads as the turning beads. Make them a different color or size than the other beads.

Ah, the world is your "erster", (Brooklynese for *oyster*), as Grammy used to say.

Chapter 4

Getting Started

• • •

TECHNIQUE BASICS
pull wisps
Hold the wool roving with your hands at least 5" (12.5 cm) apart when you want to pull some off. This distance allows the fibers to drift apart when you pull the roving in opposite directions. Pull wisps of fiber from an end. Notice that the fibers are parallel to each other.

layer the fiber
Lay the wisps down, side by side and slightly overlapping, in a single layer with all the fibers parallel, say, east to west. Lay a second layer with these fibers perpendicular to those of the first, say, north to south. These two layers of crossed fibers will provide the felt's integrity.

flat felting
Sprinkle the wool carefully with about a ½ cup (120 ml) of hot, soapy water.

Cover the wool with plastic. Press it flat it with one hand, holding the plastic in place as you use the other hand to press the water throughout the wool while pressing out the air.

When all indications of bubbles or air pockets are gone, and the wool is thoroughly wet, rub the surface of the plastic for 5 minutes without allowing the wool to shift around. Wetting your hands or rubbing the plastic with a rumpled-up wet plastic bag will lubricate the plastic and minimize the chance of moving the wool beneath. The action of rubbing is vital because it makes the wool felt. The bubble wrap alternately yields to and resists your pressure, massaging the fiber layers from the underside, doubling your efficiency.

roll to full
Place the roller on an edge of the bubble wrap and roll it up firmly. Wrap the stocking tie around the rolled-up work and tie once, pulling tight enough to make a waist in the roll and tie a bow or see How to Tie Up Feltwork, page 5.

Roll the bundle gently, back and forth for several inches. Roll it for 5 minutes, more or less.

Unroll, and reroll from the opposite edge. Continue to roll the bundle, adding a little pressure this time. Roll for 5 minutes, more or less.

Unroll, and reroll from another edge. Roll for 5 minutes with increased pressure. Unroll.

felt a rope
Lay the bubble wrap down with the bubble-side up. You may want to place a towel beneath the bubble wrap. Pour ½ cup (120 ml) of the hot, soapy water on the bubble wrap. Gently roll the wool back and forth. You may even choose to fold the bubble wrap over the wool and roll it back and forth within the fold. Apply more water, if necessary, so the wool is saturated. It needs to be wet to felt properly.

skewer method
Lay the skewer across the fiber, 1" (2.5 cm) in from a wispy edge. Brush the tips back to fold over the skewer. Roll the skewer between your thumb and forefinger (in one direction only) until the fiber grabs onto it. It helps to work close to the table so the fiber drags and pulls slightly, making for a denser layer. Continue to twist the skewer

Felt needles in foam, two stored in a coffee stirrer, a three-needle punch

between the thumb and forefinger until all the fiber collects on the skewer like cotton candy.

Lay out the next color of wool fiber. Place the wool-coated skewer on it. Again brush the ends up and twist the skewer, continuing in the same direction as before. Continue to twist the skewer to collect and tighten the wool.

Repeat using the third and fourth colors.

test for fully felted

Lift the plastic and gently rub an inch (2.5 cm) of the felt with a finger. If the fibers are reluctant to move, proceed with the next step. If the fibers move under your touch, continue to work for another 5 minutes.

towel dry

When you are finished felting, remove the most water from your work by placing it within the folds of a dry bath towel and stand or walk on it. (When I invite students to do this in workshops, they nearly always break into a little felter's jig. No one seems content to just stand or walk.) Shoes dirty? Stocking feet are fine but, they could get wet!

needle felt a bead

Roll up the coarse wool (or polyester batting) into a tight wad.

Place the wad on the foam. Poke into its center with the felt needle. Roll the wad slightly and poke into the center again. Continue to roll and poke into the center. Roll and poke, roll and poke until the wad begins to form a loose ball. How long you poke depends on the gauge and number of barbs on the felting needle, the type of fiber, and your pokes per minute (ppm).

HOW TO USE A FELT NEEDLE

The felt needle is brittle. If you put lateral stress on it, the end will snap off in the bead. Poke directly into the wool and withdraw at the same angle. Attempting to lift fiber or withdraw at an angle will bend or break the needle. If this happens, use a fork to retrieve the needle tip from within the bead by pressing the tines flat against the bead and allowing the needle piece to surface between the tines. Tape the recovered piece onto a scrap of paper or cardboard before discarding it in the trash.

needle felt dots/bumps

Here are two methods for producing felt dots/bumps to attach to felt. For multiple uniform dots, use the same amount of fiber for each.

1. Roll a small bit of fiber into a little wad, then place it on the foam and poke it with the felt needles until it holds its shape.

2. Using the pointed end of your bamboo or wooden felter's skewer, wind on a little bit of fiber as though to create a scary version of a cotton-swab. Slip the fiber off the tip and poke its edges with the felt needle held at a forty-five-degree angle.

(An additional method produces dots on the felt but, makes producing multiple uniform dots more difficult. Poke the end of a wisp of fiber into the felt. Poke deep enough to anchor an inch (2.5 cm) of the wisp inside the felt. Use the barbed end of your felt needle to swirl around in the air an inch above the place where the fiber is anchored. Catch a few fibers on the barbs as you swirl and then poke them into the felt, near where the wisp is anchored. Poke around the edges of this added fiber to create a defined dot.)

half hitch

This is a type of knot used to secure the thread when starting, or to weave your thread in, at the end.

Pass the needle under a few fibers of felt (or, when beadweaving, under a thread exiting the bead your needle happens to be exiting). Pull the thread through but not all the way. Pass the needle back through the loop of thread that was not pulled all the way through. Now pull all the way through. (If beadweaving, be certain the thread settles where you intended and not over an adjacent bead.) If preparing to cut the thread, pass through a few more beads or felt first.

crimping

Place a crimp bead on the wire, an optional seed bead or two, and your clasp (by passing the wire through the loop on the clasp). Run the beading wire back through the seed bead(s) and the crimp bead. Open the crimp tool. Allow the crimp bead to lie in the lower lip and adjust the two bead wires to lie parallel within the crimp bead. Squeeze the crimp tool. Loosen your grip and slide the crimp bead into the outer chamber, end to end. Squeeze the pliers to fold the crimp bead in half.

stringing felt beads

String the beads in the order of the layout. Simply pass the wire through the glass beads. Use the tapestry needle (or, for larger beads, a doll needle) to penetrate the felt beads. Fold only 1" (2.5 cm) of the beading wire after threading it onto the tapestry needle. Folding beading wire results in a permanent crease,

UNIFORM BEADMAKING

When you are making multiple, uniform beads, use the same amount of fiber for each.

Record the weight and fiber content of favorite beads so they will be easy to replicate.

so limit the needle to only the last 1" (2.5 cm) of beading wire. Use the needle whenever you need to string the felt beads.

before crimping second crimp bead

The quality of strung jewelry is determined as much by the following moment in its assembly as by the content or value of its components. Give this step the attention it deserves. Before crimping the second crimp bead, take the time to finesse the strung components. It is critical that there is no gap between the beads, yet, there must be enough play in the beads to maintain the chain's flexibility and ability to curve.

When you are confident and satisfied, go ahead and crimp that second crimp bead.

TECHNIQUE SAMPLER

Introduce yourself to the magic of feltmaking by sampling both methods of feltmaking: traditional wet and dry needle felting while making a bead in each method.

Set aside an hour or two for this project in your feltmaker's studio, (refer page 5). Then check out the projects.

MAKE A BEAD USING TRADITIONAL (WET) FELTMAKING METHOD

Water, wool, and a little work on a textured surface is all it takes to experience the magic of centuries of feltmaking.

have on hand

Bubble wrap
1 cup (236 ml) hot, soapy water
Towel

ingredients

⅓ oz (10 g) Merino wool top roving per bead

lay out the fiber

Split the roving lengthwise. Roll it into a tight wad.

Wrap the wad in the other strip of roving as though in a gauze bandage. Brush the tips of the wool forward to get them to cling to the surface.

felt it

Dunk the wad into the hot, soapy water. Place the wad on the bubble wrap, bubble-side up. Settling a flat hand lightly on top of the wad, roll it around in circular motions on the textured surface with light pressure for a couple of minutes.

full it

Continue rolling for a couple more minutes, gradually increasing the pressure. The wad will have rounded. If you rush the process or press too hard, the surface will crease or even become knobby.

(Despite the warning, if it happens, do not despair. To smooth the surface fibers, simply wrap the bead in another thin layer of wool roving. Place the felt bead inside a plastic sandwich bag and roll it around within the smooth bag; the fibers will felt into a clean, smooth finish.)

shape it

The bead should be a firm round shape. If it is not, continue rolling, covering more surface in circular motion. Rinse in hot water and then cold water. Squeeze out excess water. Place on a grate, towel, or use a long straight pin like a thumb tack and pin it somewhere to dry.

MAKE A BEAD USING NEEDLE-FELTING (DRY) METHOD

In the needle-felt method, each poke of the needle into a wad of fiber drags the fibers in its path toward the point. It can be used to produce solid felt in any shape and with many surface designs. Follow this recipe to create a round felt bead while trying your hand at this contemporary feltmaking technique borrowed from industry.

have on hand

36–40 gauge felting needle
2" (5 cm) foam cube

ingredients

⅓ oz (10 g) Romney wool, or other coarse wool or polyester batting

lay out the fiber

Pull off a strip of the fiber from the roving or batt. Roll it into as tight a wad as possible. Continue to roll all the fiber around the wad.

felt it

Place the wad on the foam. Poke into the wad toward its center with the felting-needle. Despite your intention to aim for the center of the wad of wool, likely the needle will come clear through. So use the foam to protect yourself.

Be careful to poke into the center of the bead and avoid pushing through the bead.

Roll the wad slightly and poke into the center again. Continue to roll and poke into the center, over and over until the wad becomes a round and dense ball. How long it takes depends on the gauge and number of barbs on the felting needle, the type of fiber, and the pokes per minute (ppm).

full it

Continued poking will compact and condense the fibers and shrink the initial wad considerably.

shape it

Continue to roll the bead between pokes. If you cease rolling and confine the poking to one area, you will create a depression in that area.

PART TWO

The Projects

Mokume Gane Beads

• • •

Mokume gane (translates "wood-eye metal") refers to a wood-grain look achieved in metal by Japanese metallurgists of the Samurai era. It inspires effects in the new clays (polymer and precious metal) that resemble a cross of taffeta with marbleized paper. Render that effect in felt.

HAVE ON HAND
Bubble wrap
Plastic
Towel
Hot, soapy water

INGREDIENTS
½ oz (15 g) Merino wool roving, cream
¼ oz (8 g) Merino wool roving, browns, rusts, gold
Acrylic (no wax) floor shield

TECHNIQUE BASICS (refer to pages 19 through 23)
Pull Wisps
Felt a Rope
Flat Felting
Test for Fully Felted
Towel Dry

PROCEDURE
lay out the fiber
Place the bubble wrap on a towel, bubble-side up. Follow the directions to pull wisps from half of the colored rovings. Pile them on the bubble wrap.

Follow directions in Felt a Rope, but only work it for a couple minutes. Then set this wool cigar aside for now.

Pull wisps from half of the cream roving and pile them on the bubble wrap. Pile the rest of the colored roving on top. Top this with the rest of the cream roving. Follow directions for Flat Felting but, before rubbing, carefully lift the plastic. Place the wool cigar on top and off-center and starting at an edge, roll it up.

felt it
Follow directions for Felt a Rope, working for only 5 minutes.

full it
Continue to roll the wool within the bubble wrap, applying more pressure now. Work for 5 minutes.

Follow the directions for Test for Fully Felted.

Rinse in hot water. Follow the directions for Towel Dry.

stiffen
Over a bowl or bag, pour the floor shield from the bottle into the felt. Let the excess drain back into the bottle. Place the felt on a piece of waxed paper or plastic and allow it to dry, which could take a day or two.

Note: Read the label. Wash your hands afterward or wear gloves.

shape it
When the felt is dry, use a sharp knife (that you will not expect to cut tomatoes with later) or razor blade to slice off a thin, lengthwise layer.

Rotate the felt and allow it to rest on this newly created flat side. Slice off a thin, lengthwise layer from the back and front. Rotate the felt once again, allowing it to rest on a newly created flat side and slice off the last thin lengthwise layer necessary to yield a four-sided felt log. Rotate the wool cigar to lie lengthwise on the flat side. Hold the knife perpendicular to the flat side and slice off each end.

Cut square or rectangular beads from this log.

Enjoy the surface design that emerges with each cut.

STIFFENING

Throughout the centuries of feltmaking, stiffening techniques and additives have run the gamut from sugar solution to shellac, from messy to smelly to sticky to poisonous. Desperation resulted in the one I now use most often. Night-owl that I am, I was in the throes of a felting frenzy in the wee hours and in desperate need of an acrylic medium. I had none. Feltmaking books I've read suggest white craft glue diluted with water. I tried it, but it produced a shine and, to my greater chagrin, a plastic feel.

Necessity being the mother of invention, I foraged for something else. Ah, under the sink, that blue bottle of acrylic, no-wax floor shield. Hmm. Acrylic. Hmm.

Worked like a charm. The floor shield has no visual impact, and it stiffens the wool while maintaining its rich, matte feel.

When you are ready to use these mokume gane beads, remember that, being made of felt, the hole in the bead is anywhere you wish. You will need to use a tapestry needle to pass the stringing material (wire, ribbon, rattail, cord) through the bead.

dZi Bead

• • •

The sacred Tibetan dZi bead is generally a plump, tubular brown agate distinguished by creamy colored bands and eyes. Believed to drop to earth by God, and said to possess magical powers that affect the health and prosperity of the wearer, the beads have been imitated over four thousand years. Throughout history, wool too, has also been believed to hold apotropaic—the ability to ward off evil—powers. Create this dZi bead of wool. Does that make it dZi^2?

HAVE ON HAND
36–40 gauge felt needle
2" (5 cm) foam cube

INGREDIENTS
⅙ oz (5 g) Romney or other coarse
   wool, brown
1/30 oz (1 g) Romney or other coarse
   wool, ivory

TECHNIQUE BASICS (refer to pages 19 through 23)
Needle Felt a Bead

PROCEDURE
lay out the fiber
Roll the brown wool up into a 3" (7.5 cm) cylinder.

felt it
Place the wool cylinder on the foam. Roll the cylinder a little. Poke all along its axis.

full it
When the cylinder form becomes firm, lift one end up and allow the cylinder to rest on the other end. Poke the needle repeatedly into the end, toward the other end. Poke until this end is firm.

Flip the bead so its firm end rests on the foam cube and repeat the needle felting on the opposite end.

shape it
Work one end first. Poke the needle into this part of the bead with the needle held at a forty-five-degree angle from the end. Direct each poke into the bead at that angle and withdraw at that angle. Always withdraw the needle at the same angle so it does not snap off inside the felt. Roll the bead so that the entire end is poked into a taper.

Similarly taper the other end. Avoid shaping the center.

surface design

Use the ivory-colored wool to create the rings and eyes that distinguish the dZi bead. Divide the fiber into sixths. Roll each sixth down your thigh or lap into a long thin unspun "yarn." Poke one end of one length into the bead ½" (1.3 cm) from an end. Poke, placing the barbs just below the surface of the bead, along the length of the fiber, and laying the fiber down in a ring around the bead as you go. Poke little by little until the entire ring is loosely secured. Now poke along the edge of the design, laterally into the bead.

Repeat to create a ring at the other end of the bead. To add the eye design to the bead, take another sixth of the cream-colored fiber and wrap it around your middle fingertip. Slide it off your finger. Place it on the bead within the borders provided by the two rings. Tap it into place with the felt needle using the same lateral and shallow pokes.

Add another two eyes in the center third of the bead, using the remaining sixth to make a swirling line that snakes between the eyes.

Lampworked Felt Bead

• • •

Duplicate in felt a multidotted round lampworked bead.
Just like the lampworker, start by making a basic bead, then
decorate its surface with colorful dots and high profile bumps.

HAVE ON HAND
36–40 gauge felt needle
2" (5 cm) foam cube

INGREDIENTS
⅙ oz (5 g) Romney wool, aqua blue
1/15 oz (2 g) each Romney wool,
    white, orange
12 yellow seed beads

TECHNIQUE BASICS (refer to pages 19 through 23)
Needle Felt a Bead
Needle Felt Dots/Bumps

PROCEDURE
lay out the fiber
Pull off a strip of the aqua blue fiber from the roving or batt. Roll it into as tight a wad as possible. Wrap this wad in the remaining aqua blue fiber.

felt it
Follow directions for Needle Felt a Bead.

full it
Continued poking will compact and condense the fibers, shrinking the initial wad considerably.

surface design and details
Divide the white wool into twelve portions. Follow the directions for Needle Felt Dots/Bumps to make twelve white dots.

Imagine an equator around your felt bead. Refer to the sidebar "Attaching Surface Design," on this page, to place the first white dot on the equator. Place a second dot on the opposite side. Place two additional dots equidistant between the first two to yield four evenly spaced white dots on the equator.

Imagine a latitude midway between the equator and the north pole of the bead. Place four of the dots equidistant on this latitude, centered between the original four

ATTACHING SURFACE DESIGN

Any shapes can be built on the basic bead by adding more fiber or fiber shapes as indicated below. To anchor the added fiber/shapes, direct your needle into the piece at an angle. Be certain to withdraw at the same angle so that you do not snap off the brittle tip in the wool. By poking laterally (less than 90° angle), rather than straight (90° angle) into the work, you do not jeopardize or alter the overall shape of the work.

on the equator. Next imagine a mirror-image latitude midway between the equator and the south pole of the bead. Place the remaining four white dots on this latitude, centered between the original four on the equator.

Divide the orange fiber into twelve. Create twelve orange wads. Poke and roll as though making miniscule needle felt beads until they are very nearly firm. Center each on a white dot.

To maintain the height of the added orange shapes, hold the needle laterally to the aqua bead and just barely poke the edges into the white dots. Then poke into the added shape laterally (from the sides) so that it firms while taking on a cone shape.

bead it

Thread the needle with any thread that will fit through the eye. Anchor the thread (see Beading on Felt, page 15), pass the needle back down into the felt and have it come up through the center of a raised orange dot (bump). Pick up a yellow seed bead and pass back down through the raised orange dot to exit another raised orange dot.

Repeat for all twelve white/orange dots.

Make another half hitch like those performed to *anchor the thread* (see page 15). Pass through the felt bead. Pull the needle hard while cutting the thread close to the work. When the needle is released, the thread will retreat into the felt.

Gemstone Felt Bead

• • •

Capture the color and texture of gemstone beads in wool.
Enjoy them as a soft, light, etherealized version of the real thing.

This project introduces a slightly different wet-felting method than the one in Technique Sampler.

HAVE ON HAND
Hot, soapy water
Towel

INGREDIENTS
⅙ oz (5 g) Merino wool roving, blues, greens
A few black fibers, just a wisp of roving

TECHNIQUE BASICS (refer to pages 19 through 23)
Pull Wisps
Layer the Fiber
Towel Dry

PROCEDURE
lay out the fiber
To create a turquoise bead, blend blue, green, and aqua fibers with a few black fibers to capture the look of the veins found in the real thing.

Follow the directions for Pull Wisps and Layer the Fiber, mixing and using all the wool.

Roll the bundle of mixed fibers into a wad. Close your palms over the wool and roll the mass between your hands in the way you would create a ball of clay.

felt it
Saturate the wool with hot, soapy water. Compress it evenly all over by pressing it between the opposing palms of your hands while trying to exert equal pressure over the entire felt bead.

Note: If pressed flat at this early stage, the wool will be reluctant to felt into a solid form.

Rewet and compress the wool evenly all over. Rewet, compress. Rewet, squeeze, rewet, and squeeze repeatedly. The wool will start to solidify.

full it
Press the solidifying wool between your palms, rolling it slightly while exerting pressure. Continue rolling until the wool is quite firm. Saturate it with the hot, soapy water periodically as you work.

shape it
The flattened profile is achieved by continuing to roll the bead between your pressed palms while restraining the circular hand movements to less than 1" (2.5 cm). Rinse the bead under hot, then cold water.

Follow the directions for Towel Dry.

Note: Here, a slightly pebbled and mottled outcome is desired. Unless you seek a polished and smooth finish, embrace any imperfections on the surface, especially if they increase the resemblance to real turquoise.

for a smoother surface

If you want a smooth, polished, and unblemished surface, try this no-pressure-at-first approach. Loosely roll up the fiber. Wet your hands with hot, soapy water and gently roll the mass between your hands. Add more soapy water a little at a time, all the while gently rolling, until the mass is saturated. Be very careful at the beginning not to apply heavy pressure; it may cause a knobby surface or a flattened piece.

After the mass takes on form, slowly increase pressure as you continue to roll. When the mass is dense and hardened, rinse and squeeze under hot water.

If, despite your caution, you end up with a creased or knobby surface, wrap the bead with more fiber and continue to roll, again starting gently and applying pressure over time.

Note: Sometimes the wool fuzzes out on the surface, even though the felting and fulling is firm. To smooth surface fibers, place the felt bead inside a plastic sandwich bag. Roll it around in the bag, and the fibers will felt into a clean smooth finish.

Felted Beaded Flower and Variations

• • •

The range and nuances of the color and shape of felt flowers
is inexhaustible. Create flowers that spring from your
imagination or capture the likeness of the real thing in wool.

Make a simple blossom and pin one on a bodice, lapel, or hat
with a standard safety pin. Or sew, bead, or pin one or more flowers
to a handbag. Embellish jackets, shawls, or sweaters . . .
the possibilities are endless.

HAVE ON HAND
Bubble wrap
Plastic
Skewer
Tie
Roller
Soapy water
Towel
Scissors
Size 10 beading needle

INGREDIENTS
1 oz (30 g) total Merino wool roving in 4–5 colors
2 g each sizes 6°, 8°, 11° seed beads
in various colors
Gray beading thread or color to
match dominant flower

MAKING STEMS FOR FLOWERS

To make stems, use the floral wire and tape available at craft stores. To
wrap the wire with tape; fold the end of the tape over one end of the wire.
Hold the tape at a 45° angle to the wire. Wrap the tape around the wire
so it overlaps slightly, pulling taut as you work. At the far end of the wire,
cut the tape so 2 inches (5 cm) remain and pull it while wrapping back up
the stem a little. Rub and press the tape into place. But don't stop there—
wrap a small amount of wool roving around the taped wire. The tape's
tackiness helps adhere the wool. Next wet and soap your hands and roll
the wooly wire between them to felt the wool onto the wire.

Make spiraling greens by wrapping a felted stem around the end of a
broom handle, sliding it off, and then pulling one end slightly to elongate
the spiral.

PLEASE DON'T PAT

Resist the temptation to pat the plastic. In every workshop I've conducted, one or more people pat the plastic. I do not know why. Patting it not only does nothing to remove the air bubbles underneath, but probably creates more. Plus patting causes some of the fiber, whose cuticle has been opened by the water, to lift. When the fiber lifts, the cuticle closes on itself with no chance to close on neighboring fibers (the defining moment of feltmaking). Patted fibers create a webby layer that barely clings to the overall felt piece. They do eventually felt, but they require more work. So, please, do not pat the plastic.

TECHNIQUE BASICS (refer to pages 19 through 23)

Pull Wisps
Layer the Fiber
Flat Felting
Test for Fully Felted
Roll to Full
Towel Dry

PROCEDURE

lay out the fiber

Place the bubble wrap on your work table/countertop, bubble side down.

Follow the directions for Pull Wisps and Layer the Fiber to cover an area the size of a saucer or dessert plate, two layers thick.

Now concern yourself with the color of the work. Do you want a green calyx on the back of the flower? If so, lay some green fiber radially. To do this, place one end of each green wisp of wool in the center of the

MAKING PETAL SHAPES

Petals can be formed by a slash with the scissors that carefully avoids the center. You may choose to avoid cutting entirely or you can make over a dozen slits to produce a flower that looks lush and multilayered, like a mum. In the final step push alternate petals back and lift the others up.

wool and allow the wisp to extend outwards like spokes.

Now flip the wool pile over and lay on most of the rest of your ounce (30 g) of wool. Enjoy the painterly approach by layering thin wisps of wool like brushstrokes.

felt it

Follow the directions for Flat Felting and Test for Fully Felted.

full it

Follow the directions for Roll to Full.

Examine the flower. Either go on to shape it or cut the flower into a shape or petals, reroll the bundle, tie and continue rolling for another 5 minutes to eliminate the cut edge appearance.

shape it

Drape the flower over the skewer, umbrella fashion. Wrap this bundle with the tie and roll it on the bubble side-up for a minute. Be careful not to succumb to felters' reverie at this moment. Failure to unroll and check the flower every minute at this stage may result in a bud that has felted shut, rather than the mature and open flower you intend.

Working the felt this way will transform the blossom from two to three-dimensions. Imagine the flower composed of many concentric circles. Working the flower this way shortens each imaginary concentric circle. Initially the flower will cup slightly.

Additional work produces a trumpet-type flower. Worked to its conclusion, the felt yields a tight bud.

You can fold the edge up, fold the edge down, fold some edges up and some edges down—in short, you can play with the shape of the flower. Does it resemble a morning glory? If the chin is pulled forward does it look like an orchid? Would it favor more petals?

When you are satisfied with the shape of the flower, rinse it in warm water. Place it between towels and stand on it to remove excess water. Reshape the flower and allow it to dry. Or go ahead and bead it while it's damp. It will dry later!

Notes: Wool must be wet in order to felt properly.

OLD OR NEW?

Cut the felt again now or refashion the flower five years from now. To eliminate the freshly cut look, simply rewet the felt, hold the cut edge against the bubble-side-up, and rock it back and forth.

FELTED BEADED FLOWER NECKLACE

Create a long, thin, supple stem using the recipe on page 83 in Fall Foliage Garland, and appoint it lavishly with many blossoms and buds using the Felted Beaded Flower recipe on page 35.

Or, make a shorter, 24" (61 cm) rope. Sew a flower on both ends or on one end and a leaf on the other end for a beautiful lariat.

Hotter water gets faster results.

The direction felt is worked (rolled) is the direction it *shrinks*.

Felt that is shaped when wet has memory for that shape when it dries.

BEAD IT
stamen
Use a loop fringe technique to create a beaded stamen in the flower's center (see Beading on Felt, page 15). After anchoring the thread, pass the needle back into the felt and exit where you want a stamen. For an inch-long (2.5 cm) stamen, pick up beads to cover 2 inches (5 cm) of thread. Either hide the thread within the felt or exit out the back, reentering the felt at nearly the same spot. Exit where you would like to make another stamen. Repeat the same fringe technique to create as many stamens as you want.

beaded edging
Embroidering beads along an inch or two (2.5–5 cm) of the flower's edge creates a fine finish. Refer to Beading on Felt, page 15.

Taper the embroidery by reducing the number of beads by one for each wrap.

The blossom is wearable and decorative as is. With a few simple steps it also serves as a lariat, centerpiece, bracelet, ring, napkin ring, table arrangement.

FELTED BEADED FLOWER BRACELET

Felt around 10-gauge wire per page 53 in Wired Felt Bracelet or around lead-free solder per page 77 in Scepter/Inside-Out Bracelet and sew/bead a flower to one end.

variations

Attach a flower to a thick and substantial stem like that of Calla Lily on page 41 to use singly as a centerpiece or create floral stems as described in the sidebar on page 44. Add a flower to each stem using needle and thread; add beads, too, while you're at it. Arrange in a vase or basket.

FELTED BEADED FLOWER VARIATIONS

Trilogy of Rings

Styles 1 and 2 require a ring with a high relief decoration supported by a shank rising from the band. Those pictured are Thai silver.

Style 3 is entirely hand felted: a felted beaded flower on a felt band.

style 1

Refer to the recipe for Felted Beaded Flower pages 35 through 38. In the center of a 3 × 4" (7.5 × 10 cm) flower, cut a slit large enough to accommodate the protruding decoration on a ring. Embellish a few inches (cm) of the petal edge in marcasite charlottes, and dot the surface with 3 drop beads. Before cutting the thread, make a couple stitches at the slit to secure the ring to the flower.

style 2

Refer to the recipe for Hatband, Page 47 to make an 11" (28 cm) piece of felt. Use strong polyester or nylon thread to sew a line of baste stitches lengthwise, ¼" (6 mm) from the edge. Gather and pucker the felt by pushing it down while pulling up the thread. Secure it with a half hitch (Technique Basics pages 19 through 23). Wrap the gathered felt around the protruding design on the ring's center. Secure the

felt with a couple of stitches. Embellish the felt flower with drop beads.

style 3

Refer to Felted Beaded Flower, pages 35 through 38.

Follow the directions in Technique Basics (refer to pages 19 through 23) for Pull Wisps, Layer the Fiber, and Felt a Rope to create a short rope about 4" (10 cm). Allow the ends to overlap while sizing it to fit. Retain the size by stitching the overlap in place with a needle and thread. Attach a two-or three-inch (5 or 7.5 cm) diameter flower over the overlap by

sewing it in place with needle and thread. Slide the needle through the felted flower to place 3 drop beads on a petal. Or Refer to page 15 of Beading on Felt to decorate the edge of a petal with picot stitch, and create stamens of short fringes in the center.

other variations

Sew one or more flower(s) on pillows or drapery tie-backs.

Place a flower in a crystal bowl on a table.

Make Style 3 ring as napkin rings.

Style 2

Style 3

Style 1

Calla Lily Necklace and Variation

• • •

This exotic plant is known for its yellow spike, *spadix,* cloaked within a white *spathe.* Wet-felt a replica to wear draped or tied around the neck or wire a shorter and thicker version as a graceful centerpiece to spiral up from the table or sit in an arrangement.

HAVE ON HAND
Bubble wrap
Plastic
Hot, soapy water
Skewer
Towel
Scissors
Knife

INGREDIENTS
1 oz (30 g) Merino wool roving, green
½ oz (15 g) Merino wool roving, white
¼ oz (8 g) Merino wool roving, yellow
1 g seed beads, green size 11°
15 seed beads, white size 11°
Eight 2 × 4mm Japanese drops, yellow-lined transparent
15 pearls, 4 mm
Size 10 beading needle
White beading thread

TECHNIQUE BASICS (refer to pages 19 through 23)
Pull Wisps
Layer the Fiber
Felt a Rope
Skewer Method
Testing for Fully Felted
Towel Dry

PROCEDURE
make the spadix
Place your bubble wrap on the work space, bubble-side up. Pull wisps from and pile the yellow fiber in a 4 × 4" (10 × 10 cm) square.

Roll the pile up and follow the directions in Felt a Rope using the edge of the heels of both hands, with your hands inclined toward each other. This tapers the ends **and** prevents it from elongating.

PLEASE DON'T ROLL

Resist the temptation to put your hand on the fiber-coated skewer and roll it as though it were a rolling pin. It *is* yummy soft fiber that *is* a pleasure to work with, but it is counterproductive to roll it that way. Doing so will actually loosen and unwind the fibers.

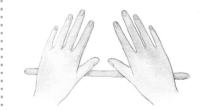

Over time, apply more pressure as you roll. When the roll feels as dense as a cigar follow the directions for Test for Fully Felted, and set it aside.

make the rope from which a spathe and bud will be coaxed

Divide the green fiber into thirds. Use an entire third for each layer. Follow the directions for Pull Wisps and Layer the Fiber to cover an area no larger than 12 × 6"(30 × 15 cm) for a decorative piece and an area twice as long for neckwear. Use the remaining third to create a third layer on top of and perpendicular to the second layer. Divide the white wool into thirds. Follow the directions for Pull Wisps using an entire third. Lay them down on a towel, covering a 4" (10 cm) square follow the directions for Skewer Method, using just two thirds of white wool.

Slide the pod of fiber off the skewer. Place it on one end of the piled green fibers, allowing it to extend a couple of inches beyond the end. This end of the rope will be worked into a spathe.

Pull wisps from the remaining third of white wool. Pile them in a 4" (10 cm) square. Lift the other end of the pile of green fibers and lay it back down to overlap the pile of white wool. This end of the rope is a bud.

consolidate and prepare to felt the wool

Pick up the edge of the bubble wrap near you and fold it back over the fiber, lengthwise, allowing the fiber to sit in the crease. Slowly continue to pull the edge of the bubble wrap away from you until the wool is rolled near the opposite edge.

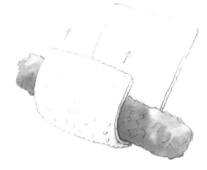

With the gentle pressure of your hands, drag the top of the bubble wrap against the wool, towards you, until the bubble wrap is barely folded.

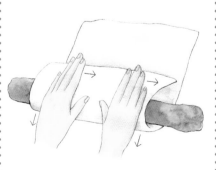

Again, pull the near edge of the bubble wrap away from you, then press and drag the top of the bubble wrap against the wool, towards you. Again, pull the edge away and drag back, with gentle pressure, and cause the fiber to roll up into a loose rope. Continue working this way for another minute.

If you want to extend the length of the stem, draft the fiber out now, avoiding the ends. To draft out the fibers, grab the rope with both hands, about 8 to 12" (20.5 to 30.5 cm) apart. Pull smoothly yet vigorously on the rope, with your hands in opposite directions. Feel the fibers yield and slide apart as you pull. Adjust the amount of effort you exert.

felt it

Follow the directions for Felt a Rope, moving your hands along the length of the rope, avoiding the end with the larger blossom.

full it

If the wool is not completely wet, add more hot, soapy water. Work evenly across the rope, except the thicker blossom end, moving the

---

FUZZY FELT?

If the felt becomes fuzzy during the fulling or shaping phase, covering it with a piece of plastic, preferably the high density kind, and continuing to work, or rub, will usually coax those loose fibers down into the surface. When the felt is overworked, as happens in shoemaking, and the fuzz becomes reluctant to smooth down, shave it with a disposable razor. Any razor you have used to shave felt should be disposed of; they are too dull to be used to shave felt again and they should never be used personally.

---

area being worked so that it sits in the fold of the bubble wrap. Increase, over time, the pressure you exert.

create leaves

Hold the knife widthwise and at a forty-five-degree angle to the stem 2" (5 cm) in from a blossom end; slice halfway through the felt, and no deeper. The flap this cut creates will be a leaf. Move the knife back 1" (2.5 cm) and create another leaf. Repeat this cut on the other end of the stem. Fold the leaves back against the stem, away from the cut. Wrap this area with a piece of plastic food wrap (now desired for its clingability.)

Continue to full the stem for another couple of minutes. This will flatten and full the leaves.

SHAPE IT

Incise the thick end of the rope to pull and work into a spathe. Leave the opposite end of the rope as a pod. Or cut a shallow incision into it and pull a small blossom from this end also. Recall the size of the white pod that you slide from the skewer, even though one end is now hidden beneath green fiber. Imagine an invisible line running along its length.

Use either a scissors or a knife to cut along that line.

scissors method

Poke the scissors into the tip. Snip. Cut along that imaginary line and avoid cutting deeper than midway.

knife method

Cut deep down into the imaginary line, being careful to avoid cutting deeper than midway.

Pull the cut edges back to create the spathe by opening it. Continue to stretch the spathe open, concentrating on the way the fiber feels in response to your efforts.

Work the skewer into the rope, about 1" (2.5 cm) deep, where the spathe meets the rope down from the blossom. Withdraw the skewer and stretch the resulting hole to accommodate a finger. Work your finger in and out of the hole as you rub its edges.

felt the spathe

Follow the directions for Flat Felting to felt the opened spathe. Finish by following the directions for Test for Fully Felted.

full the spathe

Place the spathe near a corner of the bubble wrap. Fold the corner back over the felt. Roll this sandwich up. Press and roll it back and forth vigorously for 5 minutes.

CALLA LILY CENTERPIECE

Create a calla lily following the necklace recipe, but ignore the instructions about drafting the stem part of the rope long and thin. Maintaining the stem's original length of 24" (61 cm) will keep it thick. You'll need a 16" (40.5 cm) length of 18-gauge wire to serve as an armature within the stem. Poke the wire into the stem, about 4" (10 cm) in from the end of the stem portion. Hold it firmly. Twist it back and forth while exerting pressure and driving its entire length into the core of the felt stem. Bend and arrange the wire in a large swirl. Grace the center of your dinner table with this lovely lily.

Force a tapered end of the yellow spadix into the hole created at the union of the stem and blossom.

Bring both sides of the spathe forward, folding them over the center.

Roll the lily gently back and forth on the bubble wrap to maintain the lily shape.

Rinse under hot water. Squeeze out the excess water. Follow the directions for Towel Dry. Hang to dry. Or go ahead and bead it while it's damp. It's okay.

bead it

Anchor the thread (see Beading Felt, page 18), then pass the needle back into the felt.

Whipstitch beads (see Beading on Felt, page 15) along the edge of a leaf or two.

To dot the surface of the blossoms with pearls, bring the needle out of the felt at the first desired site. Pick up a pearl and a size 11° seed bead (as a turning bead). Allow them to fall to the work. Pass back through the pearl and into the felt. Exit where the next pearl is desired.

Dot the yellow flower center with the lined drops the same way, except that you don't need a turning bead. Use this opportunity to secure the yellow center in the stem with the needle and thread.

Anchor the thread before cutting it.

Crown and Variations

• • •

This design was conceived as a crown. However, realizing that crowns are not for the faint of heart, I succumb to the prevailing wisdom that the item is more acceptable as a decorative hatband for a knitted or felted hat. Or skip the hat, add some elastic, and wear an elegant hair band.

HAVE ON HAND
Bubble wrap
Plastic
Tie
Roller
Hot, soapy water
Towel
Size 10 beading needle
Scissors

INGREDIENTS
2 oz (60 g) Merino wool roving in 1 or more colors
Nymo D, dominant color or gray
10 g assorted seed beads
4" (10 cm) of 1" (2.5 cm) wide elastic (hair band option)

TECHNIQUE BASICS (refer to pages 19 through 23)
Pull Wisps
Layer the Fiber
Flat Felting
Test for Fully Felt
Roll to Full
Towel Dry

PROCEDURE
lay out the fiber
Place the bubble wrap on your work table/countertop, bubble-side down.

Divide the roving into three portions. Follow the directions for Pull Wisps and Layer the Fiber, adding a third layer using the last third, and occupying the space of a dessert plate, about an 8"- (20.5-cm) diameter circle.

felt it
Follow the directions for Flat Felting and Test for Fully Felted.

full it
Follow the directions for Roll to Full and Towel Dry.

cut into shape
Make a 1" (2.5 cm) cut into the circle along an imaginary radius.

Make a right-angle turn with the scissors and cut continuously, staying 1" (2.5 cm) from the edge (natural or cut edge).

BEADING IDEAS

Bead embellishments any time—even before knowing how you'll use them—and then attach them three years from now!

Create the look of veins by using lazy stitch, backstitch, or couching, or adding a line of 5 or so beads at a time (see page 17). Bead the edges using whipstitch, blanket stitch, or picot (see page 18).

Extended, this spiral yields a long 1"- (2.5-cm) wide strip of felt.

FELT OBSESSION

You may be considering the way producing long strips of felt in such a compact method has just changed your life. You are thinking straps, belts, ties, and bands—all felt. You are figuring that if a dessert plate yields a strap this long, working the entire area of the bubble wrap would yield a really long strap. You might even be thinking of reweaving that Shaker tape chair with—tah dah!—felt. Perhaps weaving baskets, totes, and rugs of, you guessed it—felt.

HAIR BAND

size it

Measure the length for a comfortable hair band, about 24"(61 cm).

Cut the strip of felt 4" (10 cm) shorter.

Thread a beading needle with a wingspan of thread. Anchor the thread (see Beading on Felt, page 15).

Pass back through the exit point.

sew elastic between the edges

Exit the needle at one end of the band.

Butt this end to an end of a 4"- (10-cm) piece of 1"- (2.5-cm) wide elastic.

Join the ends with overhand stitches.

Butt the opposite end of the elastic to the other end of the felt.

Join these ends with overhand stitches, too.

Lift and stretch out the slightly curved strip. Fold it in half if necessary to fit within the bubble wrap. Roll it up and work it some more to soften and round the look of the cut edge.

embellish and bead it

Use leaves, recipe page 38; flowers, recipe page 35; or even feathers, recipe page 91, to embellish the band.

Decide whether to overlap a few embellishments (as follows), space some at regular intervals, or cover the entire length, beading as you go.

Remember that even very thin felt will hide the thread (see Hiding Knots, page 17).

embellishing the hatband

Place an embellishment (feather, leaf, or flower) on the band at the join. Pass up into the embellishment.

*Pick up a bead and pass back down into the band and through to the back side. Pass back through, coming up through the embellishment's centerline. Repeat from * three or four times, anchoring the embellishment and beading it at the same time. Feel free to simply carry the thread through the felt to exit wherever desired.

Place another embellishment on the band to just overlap the previous one.

Repeat from * three or four times, anchoring the embellishments and beading them at the same time.

Make several half hitches when you're finished. Pass through the felt and cut the thread.

HATBAND

size it

Measure the size to fit around the hat's crown.

Cut the band to fit.

Thread a beading needle with a wingspan of thread.

anchor the thread

Anchor the thread (see Beading on Felt, page 15)

When the thread is anchored, pass back through the exit point.

sew end to end

Exit the needle at one end of the band.

Butt this end to the opposite end.

Join the ends with overhand stitches.

Carved Beaded Bangle

• • •

Carve a multilayered, dense felt rope a couple of inches (cm) larger than wrist size to reveal the colorful layers within. Knot the tapered ends. Embellish the rope with beads. For a necklace, lengthen the rope, thread it with heavy-gauge wire, shape it like a question mark, then terminate the ends with bead fringe and a lampworked bead.

Note: The prevailing wisdom for a bangle bracelet is to make it 1" (2.5 cm) longer than your wrist measurement. Doing so allows it to slip over your hand. Because this bangle is made of soft and flexible felt, it's a breeze to get on and a pleasure to wear.

HAVE ON HAND
Bubble wrap
Skewer
Friction cloth
Towel
Hot, soapy water

INGREDIENTS
¼ oz (8 g) Merino wool roving or batt, in each of four colors
1 g size 11° pastel seed beads
6 size 6° transparent pastel seed beads
12 color-lined 2 × 4mm Japanese drops
Gray or surface color beading thread
Size 10 beading needle

TECHNIQUE BASICS (refer to pages 19 through 23)
Pull Wisps
Skewer Method
Felt a Rope
Test for Fully Felted
Towel Dry

PROCEDURE

lay out the fiber
Determine the order of the colored layers. Perhaps the core is pale yellow, followed by bright yellow, followed by coral, with olive green as the top or surface layer.

Start with the core-colored roving. Follow the directions for Pull Wisps to create a rectangle of wool fiber about 4 × 6" (10 × 15 cm). Follow the directions for Skewer Method using each color in order.

When the wool feels dense and tight on the skewer (like a cigar) you are ready to felt it.

felt it
Slide the skewer out from the wool. Follow the directions for Felting a Rope. Allow the piece to lengthen slightly as you incline your hands outward, the way you did with clay snakes years ago.

To taper the ends, move your hands along and off the ends as you roll.

full it
Continue to roll for several minutes, increasing the pressure exerted by your hands until the roll is firm and dense.

cut it
Use a new, single-edge razor blade for cutting. Hold the blade at an angle and make a shallow slash that does not reach the center of the rope. Make a reverse slash so that a V-piece of wool can be removed to reveal the layers of color within.

If you choose to continue to work the piece after carving, the relief of the carving diminishes and the revealed colors blend. You can stop at any point.

shape it
Rinse the bangle under hot and then cold water. Follow the directions for Towel Dry.

ELIMINATE THE WEDGE, RETAIN THE COLOR

After cutting the wedges of felt from the bangle, continue to roll the rope on the bubble-side-up surface of the bubble wrap. The more the rope is fulled in this way, the shallower the wedge becomes. Fulled to its completion, the surface rounds again. The colors of the inside layers remain as the only evidence of the excision, though the distinction between the layers softens and blends.

Tie the tapered ends into a knot. If you don't have enough to tie a knot, simply sew the ends together while you embellish the piece with beads.

bead it

Embellish the bangle with bead embroidery and bead weaving techniques. Color-lined, transparent Japanese drops magnify and intensify the light and sparkle of glass against the soft matte background of felt. Simply sewing on a few of these drops dignifies the bangle as jewelry. The bangle pictured is bead-embroidered with drops sewn into the center of the cutouts; random seed beads in singles, threes, or fives; and an occasional size 6° with a size 11° turning bead. Along one quarter of the central cutout, a fin with five peaks, five rows tall, is beadwoven of herringbone stitch. Directions for the fin follow. For general suggestions, see Beading on Felt, page 15.

fin directions

Anchor the thread (see Beading on Felt, page 15). When it's anchored, exit the needle at the edge of the center cutout. Work in size 11° seed beads, along the edge of the cutout.

Pick up 2 beads and pass the needle into the work the distance of 2 beads. If the distance is correct, the beads will situate to sit side by side with their holes up. Exit the thread on the edge, 1 bead's distance from the previous 2 beads. Pick up a bead and pass down the adjacent bead (second of the first 2) and pass back (up) through the bead just added.

*Pick up 1 bead and pass through the third bead again, tying this bead to the ladder forming on the edge of the cutout. Pass down through the new (fourth) bead and into the felt. Exit the needle from the edge 2 bead's distance from the fourth bead.

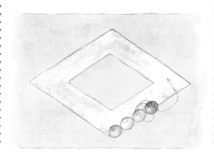

Pick up 2 beads. Backtracking, pass down into the felt midway from the last bead. Pass back up through the last bead.

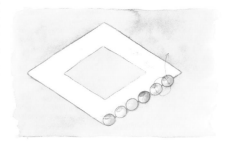

Repeat from *, adding beads 7, 8, and 9. Add bead 10 in the same way as beads 4 and 7.

Bead weave five rows of herringbone stitch off this ladder of 5 pairs of beads.

Row 1: Anchor the thread in the felt and pass back up through the last bead.

Pick up 2 beads. Pass down through the next bead of the ladder and up the following bead.

Notice that the added beads sit at a peculiar angle. Repeat by picking up 2 more beads, passing down the next bead in the ladder and up through the following bead. Repeat again and again. Now, for this final stitch of the row, pick up 2 beads and pass down through the next bead. Notice that there is no bead to come up through. You must anchor the thread by passing under the

CARVED SCULPTED NECKLACE

Mary Lou Allen has published a beadwoven necklace that uses electrical wire armature in this same shape. Mary Lou and I were amazed to both wear, independently, our separate versions on the same day at a recent beading event.

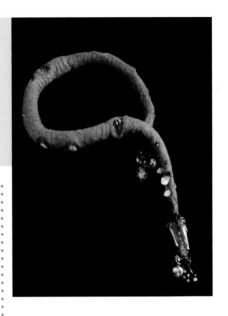

thread that connects the bottom of this bead with its adjacent bead. Then pass back up through the last bead of the previous row (the ladder in this case) and up through the last bead added.

Rows 2–4: Pick up 2 beads. Recall noticing that the added beads sit at an angle. They are inclined toward each other in pairs. This feature enables you to pass down through the next bead and right up through the following bead in one fell swoop. It is this zippity-do-dah swooping that we bead-workers love about herringbone stitch. That, plus the fact that it proceeds *two* beads at a time. The entire row is worked this way. Take advantage of the sweet, jaunty little angle the beads sit in, just waiting for the needle. Pick up 2 beads, pass down the next and up through the following, in one fell swoop; 4 pairs of beads are added in this way and then the spell is broken by the *step-up*. So, pick up the fifth pair of beads and pass down through the last bead. Having no bead to pass up through alerts you to a *step-up*. The *step-up* is accomplished by passing the needle under the thread that connects the bead you're exiting to its adjacent bead. Doing so allows you to pass back through the last bead of the previous row and the last bead added (the top 2 beads of the stack of outer-edge beads) without undoing the work just done.

Row 5: This time you want a picot or pointed top edge, so pick up 3 beads instead of 2 for each of the five stitches. Instead of the step-up, pass the needle down through the outer-edge beads and into the felt. Anchor the thread securely.

Cut the thread or continue embellishing.

ALTERNATE KNOTLESS BANGLES

Button and felt loop clasp:
Rather than knot the ends, roll one back into a loop and sew or bead it in place. On the opposite end sew or bead a bead, button, or toggle closure that will fit into the loop.

Button and beaded loop clasp:
Do not taper the ends very much. Exit the needle and thread from the tip. Pick up 2" (5 cm) of seed beads. Pass into the tip of the bangle ½" (1.3 cm) in from the tip. Pass through the beads again or weave a round of peyote stitch off the loop as follows: Pick up a bead, skip the next bead, and pass into the one after it. Repeat around the loop, picking up one bead, skipping a bead, and pass-ing into the next bead. Weave or pass through the loop again to strengthen it. Anchor the thread into the felt. Anchor a very strong thread (button thread or PowerPro fish line) 1" (2.5 cm) from the opposite end. Sew on a button or bead (using a size 6° seed bead as a shank and another as a turning bead) that will fit into the loop.

Wired Felt Bracelet

• • •

This bangle, held around the wrist by a wire armature, starts with a beaded felt bead and ends with a lampworked one. I made the first of several of these bracelets with hanger wire during a felting frenzy. If you can't get to the hardware store today, check your clothes closet for wire!

HAVE ON HAND
Bubble wrap
Hot, soapy water
Towel
Size 10 beading needle
36-gauge felt needle
Heavy-duty pliers
2" (5 cm) foam cube
Scissors

INGREDIENTS
⅛ oz (5 g) Merino wool roving in 1 or more colors
⅛ oz (5 g) coarse wool
Beading thread, dominant color or gray
10 g assorted seed beads
12" (30.5 cm) 10-gauge wire
Glass/metal glue (E-6000, Gorilla, Duco)
1 yd (90 cm) rayon or metallic thread in suitable color
Lampworked focal bead (choose hearty over hollow)

TECHNIQUE BASICS (refer to pages 19 through 23)
Needle Felt a Bead
Felt a Rope
Towel Dry

PROCEDURE
needle-felt a bead
Follow the directions for Needle Felt a Bead using the coarse wool. Then set it aside for now.

prep the armature
Cut 12" (30.5 cm) of wire. Rough up the surface a little to hold the applied wool by squeezing the wire with the pliers and rotating them so the teeth leave little scratches on the wire.

Work the felt bead onto one end of the wire. Do not press the wire through the bead. Part of its purpose is to cover the sharp wire end.

cover the wire with wool
Split the roving lengthwise. Starting at the beadless end, wrap half the roving up the wire to the felt bead. Wrap the tips of the fiber onto the felt bead. Stroke the tips until they conform to the felt bead.

Wrap the other half of the roving in the opposite direction from the bead, down.

The wire should be covered with wool now.

felt it
Follow the directions for Felt a Rope to felt the wool onto the wire armature.

shape it
Use the pliers to curve the bracelet 1" (2.5 cm) at a time.

assemble it
Slip the lampworked bead on the beadless end. Use the pliers to fold over the last ¼" (6 mm) of wire.

Wrap the rayon or metallic thread around the base of the wire loop.

Dot with glue.

Press the bead up over the glue and some of the thread; allow to dry.

bead it

When the glue is dry thread a needle with a wingspan of beading thread. Anchor the thread as on page 15.

add beads

Dot the surface with beads, embroider with beads, even add beaded fringe. The piece shown is embellished with drops that repeat the color of the dots on the lamp-worked bead.

Bead your way along the bracelet to the lampworked end, carrying the thread through the felt and only sur-facing where you wish to place beads.

Make several half hitches when you're finished. Pass through the felt and cut the thread.

Thread another wingspan onto the beading needle.

Make a couple of half hitches on the wire loop or thread-wraps to anchor the thread.

Create several beaded whipstitches to obscure the wrapped loop.

Pick up 7 or 9 beads, then bring the needle up near where the thread is.

This step creates loops of beads over the wire loop. Crowd the loops. If desired, add fringe.

fringe

Refer to Beading on Felt, page 15 to create fringes of 7 seed beads with picot tips. Make several half hitches when you're finished.

TWISTED BLUE VARIATION

Rough up and cover 10" (25.5 cm) wire with wool following the directions for the 12" (30.5 cm) wire in the Wired Felt Bracelet, page 53. Felt a 12" (30.5 cm) rope, without wire inside. Refer to Felt a Rope, page 59. Assemble as follows:

Fold over the last ½" (1.3 cm) of the wire. Squeeze with the pliers. Poke the other end of the wire through a lampworked bead, allowing 1" (2.5 cm) to protrude. Do not expect the felt covering to fit into the bead. Allow it to pucker and pleat on the wire. Using pliers, fold the protruding wire in half and squeeze it. Wrap the doubled-over wire with the decorative thread. Wrapping with thread serves two purposes: it occludes the wire and provides a "fabric" to sew drop beads onto. Knot an end of the wireless rope over the beadless end of the wire. Wind the rest of the rope around the wire, anchoring it while beading along its length. Curve to fit around your wrist.

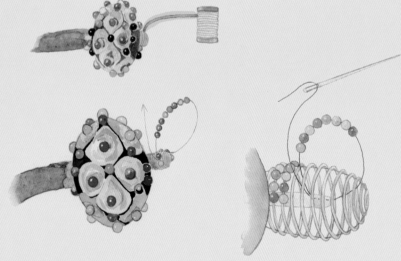

Felted Bead Diva's Lariat and Variation

• • •

Choose an actual lampworked bead to mimic in felt. It could be an ivory colored flat oval bead with black veins. It could be a multilayered dotted beauty of an inch (2.5 cm) diameter. Maybe it is a bead that resembles a mermaid, fish, or flower. Perhaps it is a miniature garden or ocean scene—the choices are staggering. Settle on one for now, and work on the remainder over a lifetime. The directions that follow offer general advice as well as the particulars for capturing the likeness of each of the two Harold Jargowsky beads pictured.

HAVE ON HAND
36–40-gauge felt needle(s)
2" (5 cm) foam cube
Scissors
Size 18 tapestry needle
Crimp tool (for beading wire)

INGREDIENTS
Collect an array of colors of fibers and yarns to decorate the surface of felt. Have that collection on hand for this project.
1 oz (30 g) Romney or other coarse wool or polyester batting, core or main color
Wool, silk, Soy Silk, polyester, nylon, and other fibers or yarns in assorted colors
48" (122 cm) ribbon, rattail, leather, felt rope, or 49-strand beading wire
2 crimp beads (for beading wire)
Any size or shape seed beads to embellish the felt bead and/or rope.

450 size 8° seed beads (for beaded beading wire style)
Size 10 beading needle
Size D beading thread

TECHNIQUE BASICS (refer to pages 19 through 23)
Needle Felt a Bead
Needle Felt Dots/Bumps
Half Hitch
Stringing Felt Beads
Crimping
Before Crimping Second Crimp Bead

PROCEDURE
lay out and felt the fiber to make the felt bead
Follow the directions for Needle Felt a Bead using either the dominant color to decorate with surface design, or choose fiber that you know will be covered completely with surface design (an opportunity to use yucky-colored or coarse fiber).

full it
Continued poking will compact and condense the fibers to shrink and harden the felt bead.

shape it
Work to achieve the desired shape. Refer to the chapter on shaping beads if your bead varies from the flat ovals shown here.

The flat oval shape starts with a soft round form. Needle down into the ball while you hold the needle at a ninety-degree angle to the foam. Move evenly over the entire ball surface that is revealed without rotating the ball. Needle the center more than the edges. Notice that the ball is flattening. Flip it over and repeat.

Rest the flat round bead on an edge and needle near an imaginary north pole. Repeat near an imaginary south pole. Flip the bead and repeat. Continue needling to attain the oval shape.

surface design

Loosely wrap the bead in the chosen fiber unless you have created it in the desired color. Tap the needle into the fiber and just beneath the bead's surface, over and over. Be careful not to pull the fiber taut over the surface. Remember that the fiber attaches by being drawn into the bead. If it's held taut, the fiber is prevented from entering the bead. Gently needle the slack fibers deeply enough for the barbs to penetrate the bead.

add geometric designs

Make the shapes and apply them to the bead. Lay fiber on the foam. Needle into the fiber many times to create a lofty fabric. Lift the fabric from the foam every few dozen pokes so that it does not work its way into the foam. There are a couple ways to achieve the desired shape. Either cut it out or tuck the edges under and needle them in place. When the shape is satisfactory, place it on the bead and needle it into the surface. Withdraw the needle at the same angle it entered. Each poke is a decision to poke straight (vertically) into the bead or laterally (horizontally) or any angle in between. For optimum efficiency, withdraw the needle only to the surface, then alter the angle or aim of the needle and poke again; repeat a few times before moving the needle to another location.

For clean edges of color, tuck the fiber ends under the patch of color and needle along the outline or border.

lines

Create lines, either fine or wide, by using thin wisps of fiber or loosely spun yarn. Place the end of the wisp or yarn at the start of where the design is to be "drawn." Poke the end deep into the bead. Notice the length of fiber that is sucked into the bead to anchor it. Just barely move the needle along the intended path of the design and poke just

---

WET-FELTING OVER BEADS

If you're using fine wool such as Merino for the overall surface color, exercise the option of wet felting a skin on the bead. Wrap the wool around the bead. Wet your hands with hot, soapy water. With a light touch, gently roll the bead around in the palms of your hands or with one hand on a textured surface. As the fibers mat and form a skin, increase the pressure just a tad. Use sufficient water to permit felting on the surface, but don't saturate the bead.

---

beneath the surface (at any angle). Again, notice the amount of slack taken up to secure the fiber in the bead. Maintain slack in the fiber and continue to just barely move the needle along the path, poking gently into the surface to attach the fibers.

dots

For some dots follow the directions for Needle Felt Dots. Sweet, tiny, little-bitty dots require only a few strands of fiber. Lay a wisp of fiber over the location for a tiny dot. Poke the fiber one third up from one end, deeply into the bead. Swirl the needle around in the loose two-thirds of fiber to capture it in the barbs; poke it into the same hole. What remains is a miniscule dot.

ASSEMBLE A LARIAT LIKE THE BLACK AND YELLOW EXAMPLE

string a chain of beads

Place a crimp bead on one end of 48" (122 cm) of beading wire.

Add 5 seed beads and pass back through the crimp bead. Crimp the crimp bead with the crimp tool (see The Tools, page 5). String 1 coin pearl, 1 seed bead, 1 coin pearl, 1 seed bead, 1 coin pearl, and the felt bead (following the directions for Stringing Felt Beads), 1 coin pearl, 1 seed bead, 1 coin pearl, 1 seed bead, 1 coin pearl, then 35" (89 cm) of seed beads, * 1 coin pearl, 1 seed bead, 1 coin pearl, 1 seed bead; rep from * for a total of 5 coin pearls. String the lampworked bead, one 6—10mm glass bead, 1 seed bead, 1 coin pearl, 1 seed bead, 1 coin pearl, 1 seed bead, 1 coin pearl, 1 crimp bead and 3 seed beads. Pass the beading wire back through the crimp bead and the pearls and seed beads and into the lampworked bead.

Crimp the second crimp bead only after referring to Before Crimping Second Crimp Bead.

Trim the excess beading wire if it extends beyond the lampworked bead.

FOR THE FELTED ROPE LARIAT AND LARIATS USING RIBBON, SILK RATTAIL, LEATHER, AND YARN:
Make a 44" (112 cm) long ¼"-(6-mm) wide felt rope to link the felt and lampworked beads. See page 87, Beaded Felt Ropes. Or cut a length of ribbon, silk rattail, leather, or yarn 35 to 44" (89 to 112 cm) long to serve as the chain to link the two focal beads.

attach the beads
Thread a beading needle with a wingspan of thread. Anchor the thread to the felt bead (see Beading on Felt, page 15).

When the thread is anchored, exit the needle at the top of the bead where you will attach the felt rope, ribbon, leather, or yarn.

Use a knitting needle, pencil, skewer, or other pointed object to poke the end of the chain into the felt

bead as you simultaneously create a slight impression.

Sew or bead the felt bead onto the chain.

Pass the needle through the bead to exit the opposite end.

fringe

Create three fringes or more, 7 beads long with picot tips. Refer to Beading on Felt, page 15.

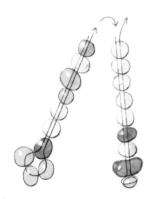

bead the bead

Embellish the felt bead with seed beads if you choose. Refer to Beading on Felt, page 15.

bead the chain

Pass the needle through the felt bead to the chain (the felted rope in this design). Stud the surface with seed beads. Exit the chain, pick up a bead, pass back into the chain in that spot, then surface and place another bead.

Work your way to the opposite end, adding (or not) beads as you go. Delight in felt's tendency to hide any evidence of thread. Thrill to

the dot of sparkle against the matte background.

At the opposite end, anchor the thread with half hitches.

Push the felt rope, leather, or ribbon through the lampworked bead. If possible, pass the needle and thread through the felt rope, leather, or ribbon within the lampworked bead.

Pick up a size 6° seed bead. Make a fringe similar to one on the other end of the lariat.

Pass back through the size 6° seed bead and the felt, ribbon, or leather, then pass back through the size 6° and create another fringe.

Repeat the process so there are at least three fringes.

Securely anchor the thread into the felt, leather, or ribbon with half hitches.

Pass through it a little way before cutting the thread close to the work.

FELTED BEAD DIVA'S NECKLACE

Create a trio of felt beads in the likeness of a lampworked bead. Felt a half dozen solid beads (and maybe even one more to hide the magnetic closure) to complement these. Arrange and string this collection of beads on beading wire.

have on hand

36–40 gauge felt needle(s)
2" (5 cm) foam cube
Scissors
Size 18 tapestry needle
Crimp tool (for beading wire)

ingredients

Lampworked bead
Magnetic closure
29" (73.5 cm) beading wire, 49 strand
2 crimp beads
22 E beads

technique basics (refer to pages 19 through 23)

Needle Felt a Bead
Stringing Felt Beads
Crimping
Before Crimping Second Crimp Bead

needle felt

Follow the directions for Needle Felt a Bead to create 3 beads in the lampworked bead's likeness and 6 assorted solid felt beads plus 1 to cut in half to hide the magnetic closure.

assemble the necklace

Follow the directions for Crimping and Stringing Felt Beads to string two E beads, a felt bead, two E beads, a felt bead, two E beads, a designed felt bead, two E beads, a felt bead, two E beads, a designed felt bead, two E beads, a felt bead, two E beads, the lampworked bead, two E beads, a designed felt bead, two E beads, a felt bead, two E beads, a felt bead, two E beads. *Remove the needle to pick up a crimp bead. Put the needle back on and pass into a halved bead. Pass through the magnetic finding and back through the halved bead. Remove the needle and pass the beading wire back through the crimp bead.

crimp the crimp bead

Slide the needle onto the other end of the beading wire. Follow the above directions from *, after following the directions for Before Crimping Second Crimp Bead.

Rose Bolo

• • •

One of the most treasured blossoms is the rose. The variety and array found in nature can only be exceeded by what is possible in felt. Felt yourself a red, red rose, one of the exotic black ones, or one drawn from your deepest imaginings.

HAVE ON HAND
Bubble wrap
Plastic
Tie
Friction cloth
Roller
Scissors
Hot, soapy water
Towel
Size 10 beading needle

INGREDIENTS
¾ oz (24 g) Merino wool roving in
    1–5 blossom colors
1 oz (30 g) Merino wool roving in
    1 or more greens for leaf and bolo
1 magnetic closure
Beading thread in green or gray
Lampworked rose center, optional
6 color-lined Japanese drop beads

**TECHNIQUE BASICS (refer to
pages 19 through 23)**
Pull Wisps
Layer the Fiber
Flat Felting
Test for Fully Felted
Roll to Full
Felt a Rope
Towel Dry
Half Hitch

PROCEDURE
lay out the fiber
Place the bubble wrap down, smooth side up.

Follow the directions for Pull Wisps using the rose-colored rovings. Follow the directions for Layer the Fiber, using about a ¼ oz (8 g) per layer. Make only two layers. Cover about 4 × 14" (10 × 35.5 cm).

Layer wisps of the remaining blossom-colored roving, like brushstrokes, to achieve the nuances of nature. For example, to create a rose whose center will be gold and surrounded by pink petals that are richly veined with maroon, place gold fibers along one end of the layered wool, lay some pinks along the rest. On the far end, create the appearance of veins by placing opened wisps of maroon fiber on the pink background.

felt the rose
Follow the directions for Flat Felting. Follow the directions to Test for Fully Felted.

full the rose
Follow the directions for Roll To Full and Towel Dry.

shape the rose
Roll up the felt from the end that best represents the rose's center. To achieve the look of a rose, tuck and fold the top edge as you roll. Don't hesitate to roll, unroll and reroll the felt until it best expresses its rosy nature. Secure it with thread.

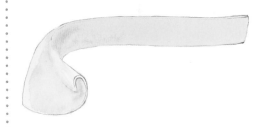

bead the rose
Even though the flower is damp, you may as well attach 1 or 2 beads to the petals while the needle and thread are in your hand. A simple half dozen color-lined transparent

beads, especially Japanese drops, look dazzling placed randomly and singly on the felt. Beads in the color of the petals are lovely, and blue beads conjure morning dew.

Do not cut the thread.

lay out the bolo fiber

Place the bubble wrap, bubble-side up, on the now dampened towel. Using three-quarters of the greens and all of the remaining blossom colors follow the directions for Pull Wisps. Lay them across the 18"- (45.5-cm) wide bubble wrap. Arrange areas of blossom color for the ends of the bolo. Fold the front third of the bubble wrap up over the wool and, pressing lightly on it with both hands, retract your hands. Again, fold the front third of the bubble wrap up over the wool and, while pressing lightly on it, retract your hands. Repeat this pressure several times to consolidate the wool.

draft out the length

Lengthen the bolo to about 3 or 4 feet (91–118 cm) by grasping the rope with hands 6–8" (15–20.5 cm) apart and pulling evenly with enough force to separate some of the fibers from others but gently enough not to separate them all. Work your way down the entire length. Check the length after one pass. If necessary, gently repeat.

Note: Recall the way we made clay ropes in elementary school. Starting in the center and rolling out toward

the ends lengthens the rope as it is worked. If you expect to default to this method, you could be better off not drafting out the extra length now. Your rope will likely reach its length during the felting.

felt the bolo rope

Follow the directions for Felt a Rope, starting with a ¼ cup (60 ml) of hot, soapy water. Work just a portion of the rope at a time. Move the rope along to work the next area within the bubble wrap. Expect to work on this at least a half hour.

full the felt rope

Resaturate the rope with hot, soapy water and roll the entire length for a minute per foot (30.5 cm) using extreme pressure.

shape the bolo rope

Rinse in hot water and then in cold water. Squeeze out the water. Follow the directions for Towel Dry. Pull the rope out straight and hang over a hook or line to dry.

lay out the fiber for leaf and loop

Place the bubble wrap down, smooth side up.

Divide the remaining ¼ oz (8 g) of wool roving. Follow the directions for Pull Wisps and Layer the Fiber to produce 2 layers covering 4 × 6" (10 × 15 cm).

felt it

Follow the directions for Flat Felting.

full it

Follow the directions for Roll to Full.

shape it

Unroll. Cut 1" (2.5 cm) or so off one side so the remaining portion is square. Place the cutoff piece on the bubble wrap. Trim the square into the desired leaf shape. This one is cut like a lily pad. Reroll and work it for 5 minutes to soften the cut edge.

assemble the bolo

Recall that the thread is still attached to the rose. Use it to anchor the leaf to the rose. Though the anchoring is done with a needle and thread and might be considered sewing, I prefer to think of it as beading. So go ahead and bead (sew on some beads) the leaf as you attach the flower.

TAKE IT EASY

If water is introduced to the wool while it is too soft and loose, it will collapse into a flat ribbon. This is not a tragedy of the magnitude of hollow bread sticks, but it's similar in cause and effect.

The cure is to quickly and firmly roll the ribbon up into a rope and resume working it.

Bead the edge for 1 or 2" (2.5 or 5 cm) using a whip or blanket stitch that carries three seed beads. (Exiting the felt near the leaf's edge, pick up 3 beads and take the needle over the edge and come up through the felt at the edge an ⅛" [3 mm] away. Repeat for six stitches.)

make the magnetic loop closure

Lengthwise, fold over the piece of felt cut from the leaf. Sew or bead one end to the back of the leaf, ½" (1.3 cm) off-center. Sew a magnetic closure into the opposite end of the folded felt, hiding it inside the fold. Sew the other half of the magnetic closure to the leaf underside, a ½" (1.3 cm) off-center in the opposite direction. Allow the magnets to attract each other. They should produce a loop that will fit over the bolo.

bead the bolo (variation, not shown)

Dot the lower several inches of both ends with beads. Outline any color patches that emerge from the blossom fiber added to the rope. Add 1" (2.5 cm) of picot here and there, (see Beading On Felt, page 15, for beading techniques).

Use the picot base to bead weave a wing of five rows of peyote stitch.

peyote stitch wing

Consider the picot base as row one. From now on, pick up a bead and enter the next high bead.

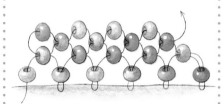

Repeat across the row. At the end of the row, pick up a bead, turn and bead across the row in the opposite direction, again passing through the high bead.

To wear the bolo, center the rope on your neck with both ends falling down your front. Open the magnetic loop on the back of the leaf and rose. Place the two ropes within the loop and allow the magnets to attract each other and close.

Wrapped, Rolled, and Ruffled Beads Necklace

• • •

A wool rope of one color is covered with another color and yet
another and even a fourth. This rope is felted until it's dense and solid.
One tapered end cut at an angle reveals the colorful layers within. Ruffled
edging accentuates the focal bead. Sliced at intervals, the remaining rope
provides several felt beads to string around the focal bead.

HAVE ON HAND
Bubble wrap
Bamboo skewer
Friction cloth
Hot, soapy water
Towel
Razor blade or knife
Size 10 beading needle
Size 18 tapestry or chenille needle
Crimp tool

INGREDIENTS
½ oz (15 g) Merino wool roving,
    4 colors
3 g each sizes 11°, 8°, 6° assorted
    seed beads
Beading thread, gray or dominant
    color
Acrylic no-wax floor treatment
Medium beading wire 3" (7.5 cm)
    longer than necklace length
    (0.019 inch [.05 cm])
2 size 2 mm crimp beads (inside
    diameter to accommodate .04
    inch [.10 cm])
Magnetic or other closure

TECHNIQUE BASICS (refer to pages 19 through 23)
Pull Wisps
Skewer Method
Felt a Rope
Towel Dry
Half Hitch
Crimping
Stringing Felt Beads
Before Crimping Second Crimp
    Bead

PROCEDURE

lay out the fiber
Follow the directions to Pull Wisps
and lay down a rectangle of wool
about 4 × 6" (10 × 15 cm) on the
friction cloth. Follow the directions
for the Skewer Method. Make the
wool denser and tighter by continuing to twist the skewer while allowing it to gently touch the friction
cloth.

felt it
Slide the skewer out from the wool.
Follow the directions for Felt a Rope.

full it
Rewet with hot water and roll with
increased pressure, then extreme
pressure, until the rope is firm and
stiff. Stiffen it according to directions on page 27.

shape the beads
For a focal bead, slice a 2" (5 cm)
segment from the end, holding the
knife or blade at an angle. Cut the
rest of the rope into beads every ¾
to 1" (2 to 2.5 cm). Seek to make
them uniform or decide to create as
varied an assortment as possible.

bead the focal bead
Bead a row of picot along the edge.
Use the "high" beads this produces
as a base for peyote stitch. Weave
several rows of peyote stitch,
increasing the number of beads in
each row so that it ruffles, as follows:

Thread the needle with a wingspan
of thread. Anchor the thread (see
Beading on Felt, page 15), then pass

back through the exit point and direct the needle to exit at the cut edge of the bead.

Row 1: Use all size 11° beads for this row. Pick up 3 seed beads. Pass through the edge of the felt a bead's width away. Pass back through the third bead.

GOOD DESIGN ADVICE

Vary the style of bead produced from one rope. Cut some straight and some at an angle. Notice the difference in the results. A straight cut produces concentric circles of color. Wonderful. Primal. An angled cut elongates the surface to yield an appearance more like an eye. Also wonderful but less primal—almost elegant.

Hmm. Could this be another food association? The bread in a pizza parlor is frequently cut straight down and served on a waxed paper in a plastic basket, whereas the baguette in a French restaurant is cut at an angle and enveloped in white linen in a woven basket.

*Pick up 2 seed beads. Pass through the edge of the felt a bead's width away. Pass back through the second bead.

Repeat from * for the desired length of the ruffle. At the end of the row pass back through **both** the second bead and the first, producing a step-up.

Row 2: Turn the work. Use any size of seed bead for this and all subsequent rows.

**Pick up 1 or 2 beads and pass through the next high bead of Row 1. The decision whether to choose 1 or 2 beads is determined by the gap they will fill to reach to the next high bead. The size of the bead will also be a determining factor. It may take 2 size 11°s to fill the same sized gap as 1 size 8 or 6. Each stitch is a decision.

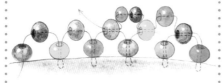

Row 3: Turn the work. Pick up 1 or 2 beads and pass through the next high bead of the previous row. Continue to peyote bead-weave between each and every high bead from the previous row (Row 2).

The beadwork is forced to ruffle by these rows of radical increases. Be fearless and full of adventure. In addition to a fine ruffle, you're rewarded by increased freedom in doing all the beadwork that follows.

Rows 4 through 8: Repeat from **.

Finish by knotting the thread with half hitches. Pass under the thread that connects the bead you're exiting with another bead. Before pulling the thread entirely, pass back through the little loop of thread that remains. Pull on the thread to force the knot into the beads. Pass through a few more beads. Make a half hitch. Repeat once for a total of three half hitches. Pass through a few more beads before cutting the thread.

assemble it

Lay out the felt beads in the order you want to string them. Arrange and rearrange them until you are satisfied.

Cut a length of beading wire 3" (7.5 cm) longer than the finished piece will be.

String a crimp bead and 4 seed beads sizes 8° and 6°. Add the magnetic (or other) closure. Pass the beading wire back through the seed beads and crimp bead.

Crimp the crimp bead. Refer to page 8.

String 3" (7.5 cm) of seed beads sizes 8° and 6°. Throughout this assembly, you may want to use more or fewer beads, depending on the desired length. Follow the directions for Stringing Felt Beads to string a felt bead.

***String 7 seed beads, 1 felt bead, 7 seed beads, 1 felt bead, and 7 seed beads.

String the focal bead. To re-create the look of the example, imagine a lengthwise line crossed by three equidistant lines. String through the topmost imaginary line.

Repeat from ***, finishing with the last felt bead rather than another focal bead.

GOOD STRINGING ADVICE

How you string a bead presents another opportunity to vary bead style. Pass through the cylinder shaped bead from the side for one look and pass through the face for another look. Create the look of a briolette, those pear shaped beads that are strung through their narrow end by stringing the beads above their center.

String 3" (7.5 cm) of seed beads sizes 8° and 6°, 1 crimp bead, 4 more seed beads, and the other end of the magnetic (or other style) closure.

Pass the beading wire back through the 4 seed beads, the crimp bead,

and several more seed beads. Refer to Before Crimping Second Crimp Bead. Crimp the second crimp bead.

Carefully trim the excess beading wire.

Compositions in Felt and Glass Beads

• • •

Assemble a dozen sparkling glass beads. Allow them to inspire the creation of eleven handcrafted felt beads. Alternate stringing the glass and felt beads into a necklace that will elicit wonder and compliments whenever you wear it.

HAVE ON HAND

36–40 gauge felt needles
2" (5 cm) or larger foam cube
Size 18 tapestry needle
Crimp tool

INGREDIENTS

12 AB faceted glass beads, ½" (1.3 cm) circumference
1½ oz (45 g) coarse wool or polyester fiber for core
½ oz (15 g) space-dyed wool, silk or Soy Silk roving, or yarn for decoration (To create your own space-dyed roving, see page 14.)
24" (61 cm) medium beading wire (either 0.019 or 0.018 inch)
2 seed beads, with hole large enough to pass beading wire through twice
2 crimp beads (with inside diameter to fit doubled wire)
Magnetic or other clasp

TECHNIQUE BASICS (refer to pages 19 through 23)

Needle Felt a Bead
Stringing Felt Beads
Crimping
Before Crimping Second Crimp Bead

PROCEDURE

handcraft felt beads

Follow the directions for Needle Felt for 11 beads in varying sizes from ¾ to 1¾" (2 to 4.5 cm).

decorate the felt beads

Loosely wind a thin strip of space-dyed roving around the bead.

For a similar effect, combine 1"- (2.5-cm) long wisps of differently colored fiber end to end.

Poke the felt needle just below the surface. After several pokes, hold the needle lateral to the surface and poke some more. Shallow pokes will cause the design to adhere to the bead without affecting the overall shape. A piece of yarn could be similarly used to decorate the bead, tapped into place with the tip of the felt needle.

Decorate all 11 felt beads.

compose a necklace

Lay the beads out on a towel or bead design board. Arrange and rearrange them, allowing the

concept of balance to establish an appealing order. Some beaders will prefer symmetry. Some will arrange the beads in a graduated fashion, going small to large to small like a string of pearls. I like to arrange beads asymmetrically, though balanced, with the largest bead centered.

assemble the necklace

Cut a length of beading wire at least 3" (7.5 cm) longer than the length of the laid-out beads.

String a crimp bead and a seed bead and the closure on the beading wire. Pass the wire back through the seed bead and crimp bead. Follow the directions for Crimping.

String the beads in the order of the layout.

These beads are strung through their center, but remember that the bead hole is anywhere on the bead.

complete stringing

Finish the piece using the other crimp bead, a seed bead, and the second half of the clasp. Pass the beading wire back through the seed bead and crimp bead.

Follow the directions for Before Crimping Second Crimp Bead.

Trim the beading wire if it cannot be tucked into the beads.

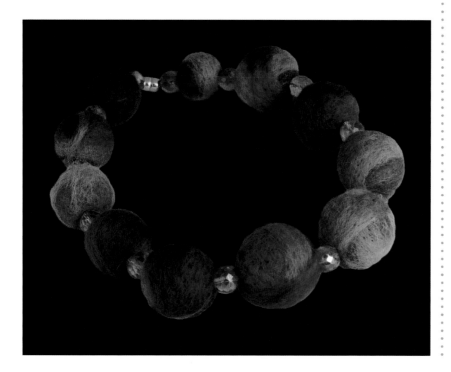

BALANCE

Consider the relative sizes and weights of the beads and how they will hang. Consider color and texture and how their placement directs the eye of the beholder. Does the easy balance of symmetry appeal to you? Then perhaps you will graduate sizes with the largest bead in the center. Are you attracted to asymmetry; are you up to the challenge of balancing such a design? The photographer's adage, "the angle of reflection is equal to the angle of incidence," may help. That is, balance an off-center focal bead by placing two focal beads on the opposite side, as shown at left.

Gemstone and Felt Bead Necklace

• • •

Moukaite is the color of eggplant and Dijon mustard, and each bead will be either of these colors or a combination of the two. It takes bits of wool in raspberry, brown, gold, rosewood, olive, orange, maroon, and ecru to capture moukaite's palette. Handcraft a dozen finger-shaped felt beads that start out as a thick rope. Divide the rope into bead lengths for fulling and shaping. Alternate these beads with a dozen smaller but similarly shaped moukaite beads. Hide the magnetic closure inside one of the felt beads.

HAVE ON HAND
Bubble wrap
Hot, soapy water
Towel
Scissors
Size 18 tapestry needle
Crimp tool

INGREDIENTS
12 size 6mm moukaite beads, finger shaped
14 moukaite beads, 10 × 4mm
1½ oz (45 g) Merino wool roving, raspberry, brown, gold, rosewood, maroon
½ oz (15 g) Merino wool roving, olive, orange, ecru
24" (61 cm) 0.019 or 0.018" beading wire
2 crimp beads (with inside diameter to fit doubled wire)
Magnetic clasp

TECHNIQUE BASICS (refer to pages 19 through 23)
Pull Wisps
Felt a Rope
Towel Dry
Crimping
Stringing Felt Beads
Before Crimping Second Crimp Bead

PROCEDURE
lay out the fiber
Follow the directions for Pull Wisps. Pile wisps of various colors of wool covering about 6 × 18" (15 × 45.5 cm) with the intention of re-creating the gemstone's colors and markings.

Fold the bubble wrap over the wool so that it sits in the crease. Gently roll it back and forth within the folded bubble wrap. Apply the lightest pressure and roll for a few moments to consolidate the wool. Increase pressure gradually as you work.

felt it
Follow the directions for Felt a Rope. Work for at least 10 minutes, with increasing pressure.

make the beads
Divide the rope into beads. Use large scissors or a blade to cut the rope crosswise into beads. Cut to any length desired. (For flat, round beads, cut the length to equal the width.) The finger-shaped beads pictured are 1½ to 2½" (3.8 to 6.5 cm) long and ⅜ to ½" (1 to 1.3 cm) wide.

This rope will probably yield more beads than you need for the project. However, erring on the side of extravagance affords choices when it is time to assemble the necklace.

shape each bead
For round beads, saturate them and roll them pressed between

your palms. Doing so will round them and flatten them simultaneously. Allow one to remain rounded for cutting in half to hide the magnetic closure.

For the finger-shaped beads, press each end into the bubble wrap as though stubbing it out. Then, holding the bead on end, rock it back and forth. Doing so will felt and soften the blunt-cut look of the fibers.

Patiently work each bead, fulling and shaping it in the process. A bead that is not fulled completely will not hold up to wear.

Rinse each bead in hot water, then cold water, then hot again.

Follow the directions for Towel Dry.

compose a necklace

Cut a small felt bead in half. Dig at the interior with the scissors tips to make a space to seat the magnetic closure. Follow suit with the other half.

Lay the beads out on a towel or bead design board. Arrange the beads in a graduated fashion with the largest bead centered. Or arrange the beads in a way that pleases you.

assemble the necklace

Cut a length of beading wire at least 3" (7.5 cm) longer than the length of the laid-out beads.

Refer to Stringing Felt Beads and Crimping. Put a crimp bead on the beading wire (see The Tools, page 8). Pass through the bottom half of the felt bead that will hide the magnet.

Pass the beading wire through half of the magnetic closure and back through the felt-bead half and into the crimp bead.

When you're confident that the magnet is settled into the felt bead, use the crimp tool to crimp the crimp bead.

String 7 small moukaite beads, a moukaite finger bead, (imagine three evenly spaced crosswise lines that divide each felt finger bead into four equal sections, string the felt through the top of the three lines, remembering that the bead hole is potentially anywhere on the bead). Alternate the gemstone and felt beads until all the fingers are strung. Complete your stringing with 7 small moukaite beads, a crimp bead, and the other half of the felt-bead magnetic closure. Pass back through the closure bead and the crimp bead.

Refer to Before Crimping Second Crimp Bead.

Trim the beading wire if it cannot be tucked into the beads.

bead the gemstone beads

Patterns and designs in the natural stone can be re-created in the felt bead with seed beads. Refer to Beading on Felt, page 15.

ABOUT BEADING WIRE

Necklaces often used to be strung on plastic-coated wire with barrel clasps that worked their way open in a few hours of wear. The stiffness of the wire prevented the beads (all but the honkingest) from hanging. Instead, the beads were held in a ring around the wearer's neck. Once inside your local bead store, you'll notice new generations of beading wire. Incredibly thin metal wire is cabled in bunches of 7. These cables are in turn cabled together. Quality ranges from the 7 strands to 14 to 21; the finest is 49 strands and yields a drape and hand similar to that of thread. It is available in various colors, finishes, and sizes. Some brands are even knotable, though you will likely prefer crimp beads to knots to secure your beading wire.

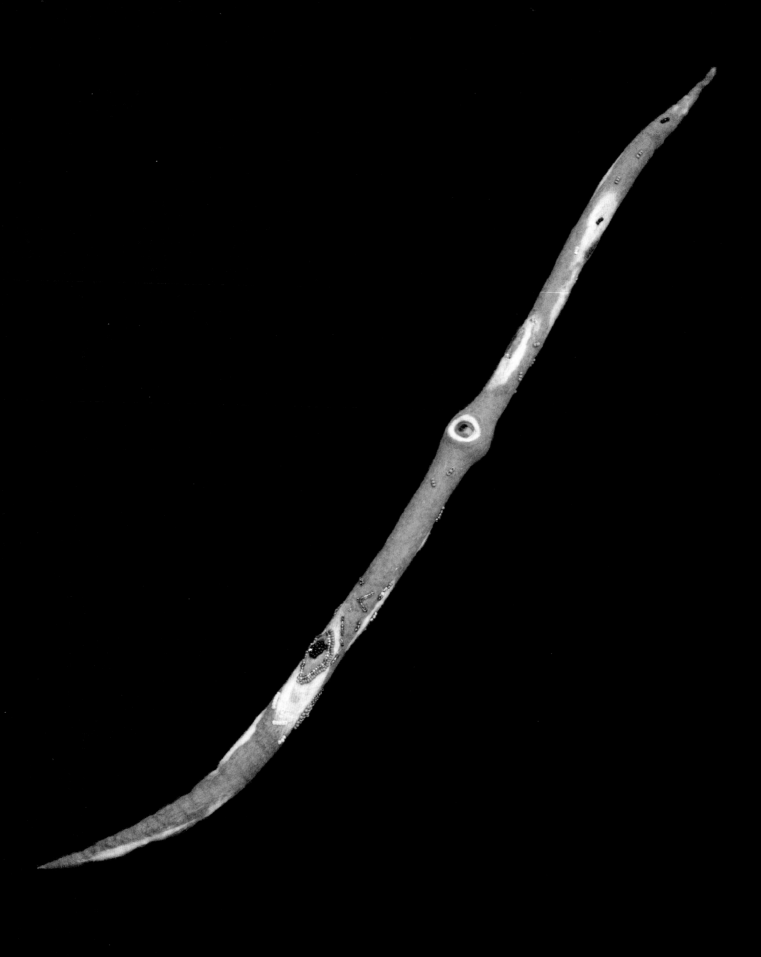

Scepter and Variations

• • •

A glass bead in felt seems to peer out. Enjoy this emblem of authority in its linear state or coil it into a bracelet that will slip over your hand. The armature within this wand is lead-free solder, which you can find in a hardware store, wound on a spool like wire. Choose the thicker of the two standard sizes. Donna Zaidenburg uses this as the armature inside her tubular beadwork to create clasp-free bracelets. I have used solder inside many pieces. Only once have I experienced the unfortunate circumstance of the solder breaking. I had opened the solder bangle by torque rather than flex movement, and this could be the explanation.

HAVE ON HAND
Bubble wrap
Skewer
Friction cloth
Hot, soapy water
Towel
Scissors
Size 10 beading needle

INGREDIENTS
½" (1.3 cm) lampworked eye bead
⅝ oz (25 g) Merino wool roving, taupe
⅛ oz (5 g) each Merino wool roving, baby blue, white, black
16" (40.5 cm) lead-free solder
1 g each size 11° seed beads, size 11° matte gray AB, opaque black, black-lined amber, matte blue, transparent blue, milky white
5 Japanese lined drops, clear, blue-lined
Beading thread, white or gray

TECHNIQUE BASICS (refer to pages 19 through 23)
Pull Wisps
Layer the Fiber
Felt a Rope
Skewer Method
Towel Dry
Half Hitch

PROCEDURE
set up the armature
Rough up the surface of the solder by rubbing it with coarse sandpaper, scratching it with a file or textured pliers, or rolling it on a cement sidewalk. Have the surface rough and the shape as straight as possible.

Pass the roughed-up lead-free solder wire through the bead. Stabilize the bead midway on the solder in one of several ways. Glue the bead in place or wind 3" (7.5 cm) of tape on the solder at either end of the bead, or wind thick thread on the solder at either end of the bead.

lay out the fiber
Follow the directions for Pull Wisps and Layer the Fiber to stack two layers of taupe wool covering 18 × 6" (45.5 × 15 cm).

Lay the solder with the centered bead on the wool, lengthwise, 1" (2.5 cm) in from the edge. Brush the fiber tips up over the solder.

Slowly roll up the fiber as tightly as you can. Fold the bubble wrap up over it. Gently roll it back and forth about 6" (15 cm) within the crease.

set up the surface design
Pull wisps of black roving and stack them to create a rectangle of wool

fiber about 3 × 6" (7.5 × 15 cm).
Follow the directions for Skewer
Method. Follow with blue wool and
finish.

Repeat using the white wool.

Continue to twist the skewer to
tighten the wool.

Slide the skewer out.

Slice the roll with scissors or knife
into slices ½" (1.3 cm) thick. Nine
slices of varied sizes decorate the
example.

Carefully pick up the slices and
press them onto the taupe wool of
the armature. Roll it back and forth
on the bubble side to coax the slices
to start to attach to the wool.

felt it
Follow the directions for Felt a
Rope.

Gently roll the scepter on the bubble
wrap until the design felts into the
surface.

full it
When the scepter begins to feel
firm, increase pressure and work it
in the way you made clay snakes in
grade school. Allow the scepter to
elongate beyond the solder. Taper
the ends. Roll back and forth with
pressure until the felt is quite firm.
Rinse the scepter in hot, then cool
water. Squeeze out the excess water.
Hang to dry; recalling that, held
vertically, the wool will shed the
water it is likely to hold when it's
held horizontally.

Slice a small wedge of wool away
from the bead, identified as the
bulge on the scepter. Also slice the
opposite side of the bead. Rub the
cut edge until it softens and rounds.

bead it
Anchor the thread (see Beading on
Felt, page 15), then pass the needle
back into the felt, exiting wherever
you wish to place a bead. Pick up 1
bead to dot the surface. Pick up 3 or
5 for dashes. Let them drop down
to the felt's surface. At the far end
of the bead(s), sink the tip of
your needle into the felt (lazy
stitch). See Beading on Felt,
page 15, for the beading
techniques suggested here.
Carry the thread through
the felt and only surface
where you wish to secure
more beads.

Continue to embellish with dots
and dashes. Outline an eye design

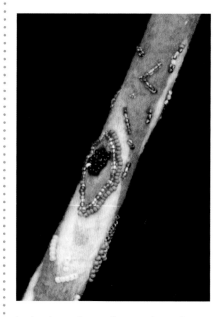

by backstitching. Sew on lone drops
here and there.

Create lines of beads like eye-
lashes with lazy stitch or backstitch.
Anchor the thread securely before
cutting it.

The bracelet variation is the green
coiled example below.

Felted Glass Pendant

• • •

Knowing that I find the effect of glass beads *on* felt completely compelling, you can only imagine my thrill at putting glass beads with*in* the felt! *Oooo*. Then I saw the glass pendants that Joe Irvin has added to his line of perfect glass beads. They are borosilicate beauties lavishly domed with a good half-inch (1.3 cm) of clear glass that not only magnifies the swirling colors beneath, but draws you into the glass to a depth that belies its physical dimensions. Felt a covering or form over a glass pendant. Cut some felt away to reveal the glass interior. Bead it, string it, behold it.

HAVE ON HAND
Bubble wrap
Hot, soapy water
Towel
Single-edged razor blade

INGREDIENTS
¼ oz (8 g) Merino wool, one or
    many colors
Glass pendant
A few silk, Mylar, metallic, or shiny
    rayon fibers or threads

TECHNIQUE BASICS (refer to pages 19 through 23)
Test for Fully Felt
Stringing Felt Beads
Crimping
Before Crimping Second Crimp
Half Hitches

PROCEDURE
cover the glass
Take a moment to examine the pendant. Is there a glass loop? Does the front surface differ from the back? Knowing these details will help indicate which side to cut open later.

Wrap the pendant with the wool. Be patient. You've got slippery-smooth glass rolling around in smooth wool. If this were easy, everyone would do it!

If you're using long strips of roving, it is okay to wet them before wrapping them around the pendant. If you are using small lengths of roving it may not make your task easier to wet them. You may choose to wind a few inches of decorative thread around the pendant, also. It is a surface embellishment and helps secure the fiber in the early phase of felting.

OPTIONAL BEADING OF THE SURFACE
Have on Hand

Scissors

Size 10 beading needle

Ingredients

3 g assorted seed beads

24 vintage beads

12 drop beads

Beading thread to fit the
    needle, color to match
    or gray

felt it

Saturate the wool wrapped pendant and roll it lightly on the bubble wrap. Roll and roll. If the wool gets loose, squeeze it firmly in your fist while allowing some hot running water to pass through. If allowed to sit in a pool of water, the wool wants to drift away. Resume rolling until a felt skin is formed. Then, roll some more. Refer to Test for Fully Felted.

full it

Plunge the felt into hot water and squeeze and roll vigorously. Repeat several times to firm the felt. If the felt starts to fuzz out, place it in a plastic bag and continue to roll it.

carve it

The felt covering should be tight and firm around the pendant. If there is a loop on top, its placement should indicate the front and back.

Use scissors or the single-edged razor, to cut into the center front. Slash horizontally to create an eerie eye-type opening or carve a coin-sized slice off the front or cut a small opening to nip away with the scissors.

Wet the cut felt and place it against the bubble wrap. Rock it back and forth against the bubble surface. Do not rub it, or it will become fuzzy. The cut edge will soften in appearance.

OPTIONAL STRINGING

Have on Hand

Crimp tool

Ingredients

20–24" (51-61 cm) beading

wire

2 crimp beads

Felt, ceramic, gemstone,

   glass, or other beads for

   stringing

Closure

BEAD THE FELT PENDANT . . . AN OPTION

Anchor the thread (see Beading on Felt, page 15).

add beads

After anchoring the thread, exit wherever you intend to add one or
more beads. Carry the thread through the felt and only surface where
you wish to place another bead(s). Refer to Beading on Felt, page 15.
One piece pictured has short fringe consisting of a seed bead or two,
a vintage crescent bead, and another seed bead or two. Both pieces
shown are studded with a drop bead here and there.

Make several half hitches when you're finished. Pass through the felt
and cut the thread.

string it

Design a necklace using the felted
glass pendant as a focal element.
Remember that you can attach the
pendant anywhere on the felt.

Both necklaces pictured are composed of wet-felted beads strung
with jasper and glass beads or
ceramic and seed beads; they
employ magnetic closures hidden
within felt beads, beading wire, and
crimp beads. (See The Tools, page
5). Refer to Stringing Felt Beads,
Crimping, Before Crimping Second
Crimp.

Fall Foliage Garland

• • •

An autumn bride commissioned wedding wear in praise of the brilliant foliage of the season. This request inspired a crownlike headdress of beaded felt leaves, a thick felt rope lavishly appointed with beaded felt leaves and seed beads that could be worn around the shoulders or as a lariat, and a scarf of gossamer-thin felt worked into silk-chiffon scrim and embellished with beaded felted leaves. This garland is one of a few design spin-offs from that wedding.

HAVE ON HAND
Bubble wrap
Plastic
Skewer
Tie
Roller
Hot, soapy water
Towel
Scissors
Size 10 beading needle

INGREDIENTS
5 oz (150 g) Merino wool roving in
   5–7 colors
Snippets of assorted yarns, optional
10 g assorted colors of sizes 6°, 8°,
   11° seed beads
Beading thread, gray or dominant
   leaf color

TECHNIQUE BASICS (refer to pages 19 through 23)
Pull Wisps
Layer the Fiber
Flat Felting
Felting a Rope
Roll to Full
Test for Fully Felted
Towel Dry
Half Hitch

PROCEDURE
lay out the fiber
Place the bubble wrap on your work table or countertop, bubble side down.

With some thought to color and outcome, divide the wool into five equal portions: one for each of the three layers, one for the surface design, one for the rope. Set aside 1 oz (30 g) for the rope.

ADDING ALTERNATIVE FIBERS

Snippets of yarns and threads, inclusions, can be incorporated in the felt. Wool ones will felt easily into the piece. You can use synthetics, even the very slippery and shiny polyamides, if you place a thin web of wool, just a tad heartier than a spider web, on top. This way, the wool fibers beneath the yarn and the wool fibers of the web on top of the yarn felt together and capture the inclusion. Small amounts of Mylar, metallic, and any fancy decorative threads can be included this way.

Follow the directions for Pull Wisps and Layer the Fiber and cover the bubble wrap with three perpendicular, 1 oz (30 g) layers. Now concern yourself with surface design and color nuances.

Use half of the remaining ounce (30 g) on this surface.

Now flip the wool pile over and lay on the rest of the ounce (30 g) of wool. Enjoy the painterly approach possible by layering thin wisps of wool like brushstrokes.

felt it

Follow the directions for Flat Felting sprinkling the wool carefully

with about 1 cup (236 ml) of hot, soapy water.

full it

Follow the directions for Roll to Full. Gently roll the bundle back and forth for several inches. If you apply too much pressure in the first minutes of rolling you will create layers within the felt and make extra work. Roll the felt gently for 5 minutes, more or less.

Cut the felt into leaf shapes. The piece pictured has seventeen leaves that vary in size from 1 × 2" (2.5 × 5 cm) to 7 × 6" (18 × 15 cm). Place the leaves back on the bubble wrap, not allowing them to touch.

Reroll and tie. Continue rolling for another 5 minutes, with vigor this time, to eliminate the cut edge appearance.

Rinse and squeeze the leaves under hot water. Follow the directions for Towel Dry. Set them aside to dry while you work the rope.

lay out the fiber

Follow the direction for Pull Wisps and Layer the Fiber to layer across the 24"- (61-cm) wide bubble wrap.

Fold the front third of the bubble wrap up over the wool and, pressing lightly, retract your hand. Again, fold the front third of the bubble wrap up over the wool and, while pressing lightly, retract your hand. Repeating this process five or six

---

FAUX FALL FOLIAGE

Autumn ushers in the electrifying transformation of foliage from green to an array of brilliant colors. Capture the variety of fall's breathtaking colors in felt leaves in several ways:

1. Hold two different colors of roving side by side. Pull wisps from their ends simultaneously and blend them.

2. Pile wisps of several colors. Pull some wisps from the pile and place them on top. Repeat. Think of the action as shuffling the fibers.

3. Recall that when layers of wool are felted, some fibers from the middle layer migrate through to each surface. With that in mind, consider using yellow or gold, the most common autumn foliage color, for the middle layer.

4. Apply wisps of fiber in a painterly fashion to the top and bottom layers of wool before wetting and working it.

times consolidates the wool slightly to form a loose roll.

Has the length of the rope increased or does it remain at about 24" (61 cm)? To increase the length, draft the fibers out by grasping the rope with hands 8" (20.5 cm) apart and pulling evenly with sufficient force to separate some of the fibers from the others but gently enough not to sever the rope. Work your way down the entire length. Check the length after one pass. If necessary, gently repeat.

felt the rope

Follow the directions for Felt a Rope. Move the rope along so that every inch is fully felted.

full the rope

Squeeze the rope under very hot water. Return to working it and add much more pressure.

Rinse in hot water and squeeze it out. Follow the directions for Towel Dry.

shape the rope

If you want a craggy, gnarled look, fold and tuck every 2" (5 cm). Use a rubber band or piece of string to secure the bundle. Give it a couple of days to dry. The felt will have memory for the bent and folded parts and yield a gnarled and craggy rope.

If you want a sleek rope, pull on it lengthwise and hang it to dry.

assemble the garland

Consider how the garland will be used. If it will be decorative, used as a swag on a window, mantelpiece, or banister, the leaves will probably be placed at regular intervals over the length of the garland. If the garland will serve as a personal adornment, will it be worn around the shoulders? If it's a lariat, will it be folded in half and worn in a lark's head knot? Or will the ends just be crossed in a loose overhand knot? Design and determine the placement of leaves accordingly.

The piece in the photo has a rope 70" (178 cm) long. A large leaf is attached at each end. Other leaves are placed at 3" (7.5 cm), 6.5" (16.5 cm), 8" (20.5 cm), 9" (23 cm), 11" (28 cm), 13.5" (34.5 cm), 17" (43 cm), 22" (56 cm), leafless until 48" (122 cm), 51" (129.5 cm), 54" (137 cm), 57" (145 cm), 63" (160 cm), 65" (165 cm), 68" (172.5 cm).

Preferring beading to sewing, I add beads with each stitch that secures the leaves to the rope. Anchor the thread (see Beading on Felt, page 15), then exit wherever you intend to attach a leaf to the rope.

Remember that even very thin felt will hide your thread. So carry the thread through the felt and surface where you wish to place beads or attach a leaf to the rope.

Periodically make a half hitch as you work. This way, if the thread or a leaf gets snagged, the entire piece will not be compromised and the felt will not pucker and warp.

bead it

After you've attached all the leaves, embellish the work with beads (see Beading on Felt, page 15). Create the look of veins by using lazy stitch, backstitch, or couching to add a line of 5 or so beads at a time. Bead the edges of the leaves with whipstitch, blanket stitch, or picot. Make several half hitches when you're finished. Pass through the felt and cut the thread.

Caveat: If you're including yarns and threads, pay particular attention to rolling the work gently at first; also avoid patting the plastic when you wet the wool. It is common for new felters to notice, when they check the work after rolling it, that the web they added to capture the inclusions has become a separate layer. This separation occurs because the webbing was lifted or shifted while the cuticle was opened in preparation for felting; the webbing felted to itself and not to the background fibers. It will eventually felt into place but requires more work than would be necessary if it had been rolled gently and not patted.

Beaded Felt Ropes and Variation

• • •

What a versatile and exciting union of wool and glass this project is. Succumb to the temptation to make several. Place a finding on a short rope for a bracelet, tie a slightly longer rope around your ankle, drape the ends of a long rope gracefully over your throat, and wear the really long rope in a lark's head knot on your neck or hung low off your waist.

HAVE ON HAND
Bubble wrap
Hot, soapy water
Skewer
Towel
Scissors
Size 10 beading needle

INGREDIENTS
1 oz (30 g) Merino wool roving, greens
⅙ oz (5 g) Merino wool roving, yellow, begonia, raspberry
2 g each sizes 6°, 8°, 11° seed beads, greens, yellows, corals, reds, browns
3 g each drop beads, yellow, coral, green
Beading thread, gray or dominant bead color

TECHNIQUE BASICS (refer to pages 19 through 23)
Pull Wisps
Felt a Rope
Skewer Method
Towel Dry
Half Hitches

PROCEDURE
lay out the fiber
Blend several greens as in the piece shown or use a solid color green. Divide the green fiber into four portions, one for each 18" (45.5 cm) section of a 72" (183 cm) rope. Follow the directions for Pull Wisps and Layer the Fiber and use one portion of green wool across the 18"-(45.5- cm) wide bubble wrap.

Fold the front third of the bubble wrap up over the wool and, pressing lightly, retract your hand. Again, fold the front third of the bubble wrap up over the wool and, while pressing lightly, retract your hand. Repeating this process five or six times consolidates the wool slightly to form a loose roll.

Note: Do not wet the ends. Leave the ends of each rope dry and fluffy.

Use all four portions of green wool to make four soft rolls, each about 18" (45.5 cm) long.

make surface design elements
Pull wisps from the begonia roving. Lay them down on a towel, covering a 4" (10 cm) square. Follow the directions for Skewer Method. Build three layers of color adding yellow roving and the raspberry roving.

Now slide the skewer out of the wool cigar. Slice off ½"-(1.3-cm) wide oval designs by holding the scissors at a forty-five-degree angle to the wool cigar. Incorporate these ovals during the felting step, next.

felt it
Follow the directions for Felt a Rope, working each of the four wool rolls separately. Work each one with a light touch and for only a minute.

place the surface design
Place some of the begonia-yellow-raspberry oval designs on a rope, more or less randomly. Accept that the outcome involves a bit of kismet. (The piece shown has nine such

ovals: one big one in the center, a couple at each end, and the balance placed randomly along its length.)

Resume working this rope, working one end and keeping one end dry and fluffy. * Move the rope along, within the bubble wrap. Butt the dry fluffy end of a new section to the dry fluffy end of the worked section. Add surface design and work this section.

Repeat from * so that every inch (cm) is felted, even those last few inches (cm).

Note: Keep the far end dry and fluffy.

full the rope

When the rope becomes solid, increase the pressure you exert while rolling.

Rinse and squeeze vigorously in hot water. Squeeze out the excess water.

Follow the directions for Towel Dry.

bead it

Anchor the thread (see Beading on Felt, page 15), then pass the needle back into the felt.

Exit ½" (1.3 cm) from one end.

Make five looped fringes around the rope.

Fringe 1: Pick up 6 size 11° seed beads (A), 1 drop, and 2 more A.

Pass back through the fourth A, pick up 3A, then pass through the rope.

Fringe 2: Pick up 8A, 1 drop, 2A. Pass back through the sixth A, pick up 5A, and pass through the rope.

Plan to place the remaining fringes between these first two fringes; aim the needle to exit the rope where desired.

Fringe 3: Pick up 8A, 1 larger seed bead (B), 1A. Pass back through the eighth and seventh A. Pick up 6A, and pass through the rope.

Fringe 4: Pick up 9A, 1 drop, 2A. Pass back through seventh A. Pick up 6A, and pass through the rope.

Fringe 5: Pick up 9A, 1 drop, 1A. Pass back through the eighth A. Pick up 7A, and pass into the felt.

Make a half hitch here. If the fringe gets caught in a door and pulled off, the rest of the beadwork will not be compromised.

Bead your way along the entire rope to make five loops of 12A off the far end.

Along the way use one or more techniques for surface embellishment, Refer to Beading on Felt, page 15.

Anchor the thread with half hitches before cutting it.

SPIRALING ROPE VARIATION

Fiber Orientation

The process of wet felting depends on the fibers locking together. This occurs when the mingled fibers' cuticles (shingle-like scales on the surface of wool fiber) catch on nearby fibers while closing. Crossed fibers are afforded greater opportunity to lock than parallel fibers.

Upon completing this Spiraling Rope project (the only one here with basically parallel fibers), compare how it differed from other projects you've completed.

Split the roving lengthwise for this 36"- (91.5-cm) long, thin rope. Lay the five colors side by side.

Have on Hand

Bubble wrap

Hot, soapy water

Skewer

Towel

Scissors

Size 10 beading needle

Ingredients

⅓ oz (10 g) Merino wool roving, split lengthwise, seafoam, coral, raspberry, white, gold

10" (25.5 cm) 20-gauge wire

1 g each size 11° seed beads, aqua,
   coral, maroon, yellow

14 drop beads, yellow lined, coral lined

13 lampworked beads, M&M size

1 twisted, transparent, raspberry, gold,
   and aqua Olive Glass tube bead
   (see Resources, page 119)

Beading thread, gray or dominant
   bead color

Hypo-cement glue

Technique Basics (refer to pages 19 through 23)

Pull Wisps

Felt a Rope

Skewer Method

Towel Dry

Half Hitches

lay out the fiber

Arrange the long, thin strips of roving side by side, 30" (76.5 cm), extending beyond the bubble wrap.

felt it

Follow the directions for Felt a Rope.

full it

Work each area of the rope vigorously for 10 minutes until it feels solid and firm. Gently pull the rope, with hands at least 8" (20.5 cm) apart, checking that no fibers slide.

assemble it

Cut 4" (10 cm) from one end of the rope.

Push 5" (12.5 cm) of 20-gauge wire into the cut piece (1" [2.5] cm of the wire protrudes). Place the end that has wire protruding from it into the glass tube bead. Secure it with glue applied with the hypo point. Push 4" (10 cm) of the other 5" (12.5 cm) of wire into one end of the rope, allowing 1" (2.5 cm) of the wire to protrude.

Push this wired end of the rope into the empty end of the glass tube bead. Secure it with glue applied with the hypo point into the tube bead.

Refer to Beading on Felt, page 15 using needle and thread to embellish the rope with beads.

Embellish the end of the rope that is opposite the tube bead by dotting it

with 11 lampworked beads. Add assorted seed beads here and there.

Embellish the tube bead end with the remaining 2 lampworked beads and assorted seed beads.

shape it

When the glue has dried, wrap the wire sections of the rope around a pen or use pliers to create a twist that continues from both ends of the twisted glass tube bead.

wear it

There are two ways to wear this piece.

1. Allow the rope end to hang vertically through the twisted tube bead.

2. Hold the twisted tube bead horizontally and drape the rope across the twisted tube bead to cross the rope ends.

Felted Feathers

• • •

Wear a simple, single felted feather on a hat. Combine it with bits of tulle and ribbon and wear it as a brooch. Substitute feathers for the foliage and flowers in necklaces, lariats, hatbands, and garlands. Use thick feathers in place of felt beads in necklaces.

HAVE ON HAND
Bubble wrap
Bamboo skewer
Friction cloth
Hot, soapy water
Towel
Scissors
Size 10 beading needle

INGREDIENTS
¼ oz (8 g) Merino wool roving, teal, sea foam, cobalt, rosewood, gold, olive
3 g size 11° assorted seed beads
Beading thread, gray or dominant color
Pipe cleaner

TECHNIQUE BASICS (refer to pages 19 through 23)
Pull Wisps
Layer the Fiber
Skewer Method
Felt a Rope
Roll to Full
Towel Dry

PROCEDURE
design the feather
Follow the directions for Pull Wisps and Layer the Fiber for the centermost color. Lay down a rectangle of teal fiber about 4 × 4" (10 × 10 cm) on the friction cloth. Follow the directions for Skewer Method, including all 6 colors/layers. Twist until it is firm. Slide the skewer out.

felt it
Follow the directions for Felt a Rope. Incline your hands inward while you roll to prevent the rope from elongating and thinning. Try to maintain a width of about 2" (5 cm).

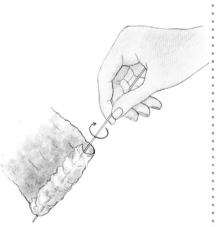

Work the piece for at least 10 minutes.

Squeeze, do not wring, the water out.

cut out the feather design

Holding the scissors at an angle, and starting about 1" (2.5 cm) in from an end, cut off slices every ½" (1.3 cm); cut to within 1" (2.5 cm) of the far end.

full the feathers

Place them on the bubble wrap, smooth side up. Prevent them from touching. Follow the directions for Flat Felting. Work vigorously.

Note: The trade-off for durable feathers is blurring of the distinct layers. Depending on how you will use the feather, consider applying acrylic floor shield on less fulled feathers to maintain clean lines between the layers. Finish the feather and refer to Mokume Gane Bead procedure to *stiffen*, page 27.

finish each feather

Rinse the feathers vigorously under hot water. Squeeze out the water. Follow the directions for Towel Dry.

bead them

Refer to Beading on Felt, page 15. Anchor the thread (See Beading on Felt, page 15).

sewing/beading

Lazy stitch a quill up the center and bead an edging of whipstitch, blanket stitch, or picot. Refer to Beading on Felt, pages 15, for instructions.

BEADED EDGINGS

For whipstitch, blanket stitch, and picot, refer to p. 18.

GOOD FEATHERING ADVICE

Cutting the rope into $1/2$" (1.3 cm) slices has produced very short fibers. Though slightly felted, they are not very stable. By working the fibers thoroughly during the fulling stage, the feathers will develop the integrity necessary to endure frequent wear.

PAINTING FEATHERS

In an attempt to capture the luminous and slightly metallic look of peacock feathers, paint bands of metallic acrylic. Jacquard's Lumiere is a light-body metallic acrylic that is flexible, permanent, lightfast, and drycleanable; it's available in 2.25 oz (70 ml) jars in many metallic colors. I used 554 Sunset gold here.

QUILL FOR THE FEATHER (OPTIONAL)

Pull fine, thin wisps of fiber and line them up side by side for the length of the pipe cleaner. Lay the pipe cleaner across the edge and brush the tips of the fiber up over the pipe cleaner as in Skewer Method. Work as in Felt a Rope.

Attach the feather to its quill with a needle and thread.

Winged and Felted Glass Beads

• • •

Beaded felted beads by another name. Just another manifestation of how glass and felt enhance each other exponentially when they're paired.

Marbles, especially cat's eye versions; 2"- (5-cm) long clear glass drops that decorate a chandelier; glass pebbles from the craft store: felt them all. Lampworker Robert Michael Croft makes small flowers and other organic shapes that he describes as implosions inside ½" (1.3 cm) rounds of glass. I love to felt and bead these treasures.

HAVE ON HAND
Bubble wrap
Hot, soapy water
Towel
Single-edged razor blade
Scissors
Size 10 beading needle

INGREDIENTS
¼ oz (8 g) Merino wool, one or
    many colors
3 glass marbles, pebbles, or beads
3 g size 8° seed beads, matte any
    color
1 g size 11° seed beads, any color
    opaque
10 drop beads
Beading thread to fit the needle,
    color to match or gray

PROCEDURE
cover the glass
Divide the wool into thirds, one third per glass marble, pebble, or bead. Refer to the procedure for covering the glass in Felted Glass Pendant, page 79.

felt it
Refer to page 80, Felted Glass Pendant paragraph *felt it.*

full it
Refer to page 80, Felted Glass Pendant paragraph *full it.*

carve it
Read paragraph *carve it* on page 80, Felted Glass Pendant.

Do not cut away more than half or the marble will pop out.

bead the felted bead
Anchor the thread (see Beading on Felt, page 15), then pass the needle back into the felt.

add beads
Imagine a line drawn around the marble, ¼" (6 mm) in from the edge of the felt. *Bring the needle to the surface anywhere on that line.

Pick up 2 size 8° seed beads.

Pass into the felt, on the imaginary line, a little less than 2 bead's distance away.

Repeat from * until crowded and tilted pairs of beads cover the imaginary line.

Pass up through the felt and one of these beads.

Bead weave a round of herringbone using double the usual amount of beads.

**Pick up 4 size 8° beads.

Pass down into the next bead (the other in this pair) and up through the following bead.

Repeat from ** until you approach the last pair of beads.

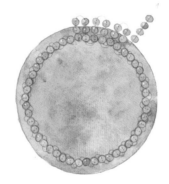

Pick up 4 beads and pass down through the next bead (the other in this pair) and up through the following one and the 2 new beads stacked on top of it.

Bead weave a round using 3 beads to produce points:

***Pick up 3 size 11° sparkly beads.

Pass down through the 2-bead stack (of this pair of stacks) and pass up through the next 2-bead stack.

Note: If there is space between the petals, pick up a bead before passing up through the next 2-bead stack.

Continue from *** until you approach the last pair of stacked beads.

Pick up 3 beads and pass down through the 2-bead stack and into the felt.

Imagine a line drawn ⅛" (3 mm) from the cut edge.

Place a drop or 3 size 11° opaque seed beads one at a time along this line.

When you're finished, anchor the thread as before. Then pass the needle back through the felt and cut the thread close to the work where it surfaces.

Spiral Earrings

• • •

Perhaps the most resonant of symbols, the spiral reminds us of continuity, of centeredness, of cycling and recycling without repeating, ever the same but different. Felt at its most delicate, these lightweight lovelies could easily blow away if they weren't tethered to an earlobe.

HAVE ON HAND
Bubble wrap
Hot, soapy water
Towel
Skewer or knitting needle
Scissors
Size 10 beading needle
Needle-nose pliers

INGREDIENTS
⅟₁₅ oz (2 g) Merino wool roving, apple green
3 g size 11° assorted seed beads
Beading thread, gray or dominant color
2 pipe cleaners
Thread, metallic, silk, or holographic (optional)
2 ear wires or posts with loops
2 soldered jump rings

TECHNIQUE BASICS (refer to pages 19 through 23)
Pull Wisps
Skewer Method
Felt a Rope
Towel Dry

PROCEDURE
lay out the wool
Refer to Pull Wisps and Skewer Method to cover the pipe cleaner with wool.

If you've chosen to incorporate fancy threads, wrap them around the pipe cleaner like a barber-pole stripe.

felt it
Follow the directions for Felt a Rope for 5 minutes. Rinse in hot water.

Follow the directions for Towel Dry.

shape it
Hold the end of the pipe cleaner against the skewer or knitting needle.

Wrap the pipe cleaner around it.

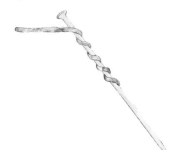

Slide the coiled pipe cleaner off.

Pull it gently to elongate the spiral.

Cut in half or to size.

attach the jump rings
Refer to Beading on Felt, page 15 to anchor the thread.

Sew a jump ring to the end of the spiral that will be attached to the ear wire/post. Simply use a couple of overhand stitches. Make two half hitches.

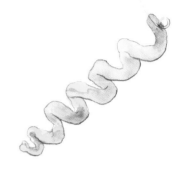

bead them

Refer to Beading on Felt, page 15 to embellish the surface with lines of lazy stitch and bead dots and to fringe the tips.

attach to ear wire/post

Use the needle-nose pliers to open the earring loop.

Place the jump ring on the loop.

Close the loop with the pliers.

Do so for both earrings.

Note: It is important to open the loop with a torque motion rather than pulling it open.

Bracelet of Swirled Felt Beads

• • •

An otherwise unsatisfying encounter with polymer clay inspired the way these beads are made. Layers of wool are rolled up, felted, and sliced to produce swirled-felt beads. String them alternately with pairs of E beads and finish with a powerful magnetic closure.

HAVE ON HAND
Bubble wrap
Skewer
Towel
Hot, soapy water
Crimp tool
Size 18 tapestry or chenille needle
Razor blade or knife

INGREDIENTS
¼ oz (7.5 g) Merino wool roving or
    batt, in 3 colors
16 size E seed beads, opaque
2 sterling silver crimp beads, 2mm
10" (25.5 cm) beading wire, medium
    (0.018 or 0.019 inch)
Magnetic or other closure
Acrylic no-wax floor shield

TECHNIQUE BASICS (refer to pages 19 through 23)
Skewer Method
Felt a Rope
Towel Dry
Crimping
Stringing Felt Beads
Before Crimping Second Crimp
    Bead

PROCEDURE
lay out the fiber
Determine the order of the colored layers. Perhaps one layer is begonia followed by pale pink topped with bright green.

Note: Choose colors that will remain distinct when they're layered. Layers that are similar in value may become muddy or blurred. Use this image to dictate your choices: would a photocopy of your three colors made on a black-and-white copier show three distinct areas or one gray patch?

Cover 4 × 3" (10 × 7.5 cm) on the bubble wrap, bubble-side up with one color of wool. Lay the next color of wool fiber on the first layer. Repeat with the third color.

Refer to the Skewer Method for how to roll up the wool on the skewer, but roll all three layers at once, not one color at a time.

felt it
Slide the skewer out from the wool. Follow the directions for Felt a Rope. Work the rope for at least a half hour, with increasing intensity.

full it
Work the piece until it's firm and dense. Rinse in hot water. Squeeze out excess water.

cut it
Using a new single-edge razor blade or sharp knife that you don't mind sacrificing to your felting studio, slice straight through every ½" (1.3 cm).

adding medium
Saturate the beads with the acrylic floor shield. Squeeze the excess back into the bottle. Allow the beads to dry. If you prefer, finish the bracelet and then add the medium.

assemble it

Lay the beads out on a towel or bead design board. Arrange them in a pleasing order and to the proper length.

Cut a length of beading wire at least 3" (7.5 cm) longer than necessary. Use it to string a crimp bead, 2 E beads, and the closure. Pass back through the 2 E beads and the crimp bead.

Follow the directions for Crimping and Stringing Felt Beads.

String a felt bead, 2 E beads, and a felt bead; duplicate this sequence for all 6 felt beads. Pick up a crimp bead, 2 E beads (or 4 E beads if you like), and the other side of the closure. Pass back through the 2 E beads and the crimp bead.

Refer to Before Crimping the Second Crimp Bead.

Trim the beading wire.

VARIATION

Roll up two or three colors of wool, as above. Make three of these rolls using different combinations.

Roll up just black wool.

Roll up just white wool.

Bundle the five rolls, lengthwise.

Wrap aqua (or your choice) wool around the bundle.

Wrap with white wool.

Wrap with aqua wool.

Felt, slice, add medium, and string following the directions above.

Or make 8 felted beads and omit the E beads between them, as shown in the variation here. Use 2 E beads at each side of closure.

Beaded Felt Pod

• • •

This primal and organic shape is enticing when it's rendered in felt. Dot the surface with the intense shine of glass, create a colorful interior revealed by an angled slash, and embellish unabashedly with ruffles and Swarovski crystals. Wear a single one as a brooch or string one or more as felt beads.

HAVE ON HAND
Bubble wrap
Bamboo skewer
Friction cloth
Hot, soapy water
Towel
Scissors
Size 10 beading needle

INGREDIENTS
½ oz (15 g) total Merino wool roving, maroon, purple, blue, gold
3 g size 11° assorted seed beads
Thirteen 4mm Swarovski bicone crystals
12 Japanese drop beads
Beading thread, gray or dominant color
1" (2.5 cm) 18–24-gauge craft wire

TECHNIQUE BASICS (refer to pages 19 through 23)
Pull Wisps
Skewer Method
Felt a Rope
Towel Dry
Half Hitches

PROCEDURE
arrange the interior
Follow the directions for Pull Wisps and lay down the maroon and blue wool to cover a space no larger than 4 × 4" (10 × 10 cm) on the friction cloth. Place the purple roving across it haphazardly, neither diagonal nor lengthwise. Using the Skewer Method, collect the fiber on the skewer. Collect the layer of gold wool. When it is firm and solid, remove the skewer.

felt it
Follow the directions for Felt a Rope with your hands inclined inward while you roll to maintain the length and width of the form. Work the piece for at least 10 minutes.

full it
Squeeze under hot running water. Work it for another 10 minutes, vigorously.

Squeeze the water out. Towel Dry.

cut to reveal the colorful core
It would be understandable if you admire the form as is and do not wish to cut into it or otherwise alter it. Simply embellish it with a few beads and enjoy. Or, holding the scissors at an angle (think quill tip versus blunt cut) cut through the pod.

bead embellish
Refer to Beading on Felt, page 15 to anchor the thread and embellish with beads.

picot foundation and peyote ruffle
Regard the cut edge as a watch face and allow the needle to exit at 5 o'clock. Perform picot stitch along the edge of the face up to 10 o'clock. Follow the directions found in *bead the focal bead* of Wrapped, Rolled, and Ruffled Beads Necklace, page 67.

Lazy stitch

Work a line of 3-bead wide lazy stitch from the 10 o'clock area of the edge of the face up to the tip of the pod, using 3 beads at a time, poke an inch of wire into the tip and bend it into a crook.

Short Crystal Fringes

Bring the needle out of the pod ½" (1.3 cm) from the tip, behind the line of lazy stitch.

*Pick up a crystal and a seed bead.

Pass back through the crystal and into the pod.

Bring the needle out ¹⁄₁₆" (2 mm) from the previous crystal, just behind the lazy stitches.

Repeat from * using all the crystals.

Make several half hitches to secure the thread before cutting.

Silk Scarf with Felt Medallions

• • •

Some industrially produced felt contains scrim (an open weave fabric that wool is felted into). Hand-felted gossamer-thin, very lightweight felt is made by felting wool into open-weave fabrics such as silk chiffon, cotton voile, various laces, and gauzes. This recipe focuses on felting areas of wool onto background fabric. Here the felting is surface design.

HAVE ON HAND
Bubble wrap
3 sheets plastic
Roller
Skewer
Hot, soapy water
Towel
Scissors
Size 10 beading needle

INGREDIENTS
90 × 12" (229 × 30.5 cm) silk
   chiffon
¼ oz (8 g) Merino wool roving for
   each of 4 or 5 colors
10 g size 8° seed beads, 6 colors
Beading thread, gray or dominant
   color

TECHNIQUE BASICS (refer to pages 19 through 23)
Pull Wisps
Layer the Fiber
Skewer Method
Flat Felting
Roll to Full
Towel Dry
Half Hitch

PROCEDURE

make the medallions/surface design
Follow the directions for Pull Wisps, Layer the Fiber, and Skewer Method to produce a 4 or 5 layered cigar of wool.

cut out the design
Slide the skewer out of the wool. Holding the scissors at an angle, and starting about 1" (2.5 cm) in from an end, cut off slices every ½" (1.3 cm) to within 1" (2.5 cm) of the far end.

lay out the scarf
Place the bubble wrap on your work table or countertop, bubble-side down. Lay an end of the silk chiffon across it. Place half the medallions where you'd like them.

Note: When you're felting wool to a fabric, start with cool water. Hot water felts the wool to itself before it has the opportunity to work into the weave of the fabric.

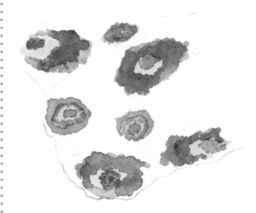

Pour some cool, soapy water on the medallions. Cover with plastic. Rub each of the medallions for a couple of minutes.

Lift the opposite end of the scarf and carry it 12" (30.5 cm) beyond the bubble wrap. Lay the second piece of plastic down. Fold that last 12" (30.5 cm) back and lay it on top of the plastic. Decorate it with the remaining medallions. Saturate them with cool, soapy water. Cover them with the third piece of plastic. Rub the medallions for a couple of minutes each. Use pressure but do not move and shift the wool.

felt it

Follow the directions for Roll to Full.

Examine the back side of the felted areas of fabric. If you see that wool fibers have worked their way through the weave to this side, you may proceed with the next step. If there is no evidence of wool on the back side yet, continue to roll. This time have no mercy. Roll with vigor and pressure. Succumb to the temptation to use your foot!

slam and shock it

Unroll the bubble wrap. Maintaining the layers, lift and place the silk and plastic contents inside a plastic bag. Press the air out of the bag and fold the edge over. Grasp one edge of the bag with one hand. Grasp the opposite edge with your other hand.

Hold the bag horizontal to the table. Bring the bag down toward the table. When you're within 24" (60 cm) of the table, release the bag with force, propelling it flat onto the table. Okay. Try again with much more force. Wham! Again, harder.

rinse it

Remove the bag. Rinse and squeeze the decorated ends of the scarf under hot water. Change to cold water. Repeat in hot water. Crumble the wet cloth into a ball and throw it hard against the table or floor several times. Put it in a plastic bag if you are concerned about splashing. Rinse again in hot and then cold water.

dry it

Follow the directions for Towel Dry.

bead the scarf ends

Anchor the thread (see Beading on Felt, page 15).

weave an edge of interlocking swags

Adapt a South African, Xhosa, beadwork technique that creates a double series of intertwined swags across the edge of the scarf.

Pick up 10 size 8° seed beads (2x, 2y, 2z, 2y, 2x).

Make a small stitch into the edge ⅓" (8 mm) away.

Pass back through the last 2 beads (2x).

*Pick up 2y, 2z, 2y, 2x.

Make a small stitch into the edge ⅓" (8 mm) away.

Pass back through the last 2x.

Repeat from * until you reach the opposite corner.

Make a small stitch into the edge ⅙" (4 mm) away.

Pick up 10 size 8° seed beads (2a, 2b, 2c, 2b, 2a).

Allow this swag to lie over the last swag, then pass under and behind the following swag.

Make a small stitch into the scarf's edge in the center of the swag.

Pass back through the previous and last 2a.

**Pick up 2b, 2c, 2b, 2a.

Allow this swag to lie over the preceding row's swag. Then pass under and behind the next swag to make a small stitch into the scarf's edge, mid-swag.

Pass back through the last 2a.

Repeat from ** until you reach the corner of the scarf.

Anchor the thread.

Repeat this edging on the opposite edge of the scarf.

Felted Silk Jabot

• • •

Exploit the way that wool puckers, shirrs, and manipulates the scrim into which it is felted. Soft and warm as breath, and guaranteed to keep a chill at bay, this refined neckwear has a delicacy and daintiness not usually associated with felt.

HAVE ON HAND
Bubble wrap
3 sheets plastic
60 × 20" (152.5 × 51 cm) plastic can liner
Roller
Skewer
Hot, soapy water
Towel
Scissors
Size 10 beading needle

INGREDIENTS
60 × 10" (152.5 × 25.5 cm) silk chiffon
2 oz (60 g) total Merino wool roving, any colors

TECHNIQUE BASICS (refer to pages 19 through 23)
Pull Wisps
Flat Felting
Roll to Full
Towel Dry
Half Hitch

PROCEDURE
lay out the fiber
Lay the plastic out. Place the silk chiffon fabric (scrim) on the plastic, lengthwise. Line up the lengthwise edges of the scrim and plastic, leaving half of the plastic bare (as it is twice as wide as the silk).

Follow the directions for Pull Wisps and place 1 oz (30 g) of wool wisps down the 60" (152.5 cm) midline of the silk, 4" (10 cm) wide.

Fold the bare half of the plastic over the scrim, lengthwise, and flip the plastic/silk and wool/plastic "sandwich" upside-down.

Fold the plastic back away, revealing the undecorated underside of scrim. Place the remaining wisps of wool along the 60" (152.5 cm) midline, about 4" (10 cm) wide.

FELTING ON SCRIM
When you're felting on fabric (scrim), pay no particular attention to the orientation of the fibers. The scrim provides all of the resulting textile's integrity and the wool is simply surface design. The wool provides color and texture, substance and warmth. Pristine areas of scrim bordered by areas that are felted into, pucker and smock in a most appealing way. The contrast of these two areas in a single textile enhance and underscore the distinctive properties of each.

felt it

Sprinkle the wool with a cup of (240 ml) cool soapy water.

Fold the plastic back over the wool covered scrim.

Rub the surface for a few minutes.

fold the work into thirds

Lift one end of the scrim/plastic and bring it over and past the center. Repeat on the other end, folding the work to occupy a third of the space.

full it

Place this bundle on the bubble wrap with the folded edges on the north and south and the open edges on the east and west.

Follow the directions for Roll to Full, confining the roller to the north or south edges of the bubble wrap. Work with increasing vigor for 30 minutes, or until the length shrinks to about 45" (114.5 cm).

cut it

Use scissors to cut up the center lengthwise, from one end to within 2" (5 cm) of the opposite end.

slam and shock it

Follow the directions for *slam and shock it, rinse it and dry it* as in Silk Scarf with Felt Medallions, page 105.

The finished jabot is likely to have shrunk to 32" (81.5 cm).

bead the jabot

Refer to Beading on Felt, page 15. Bead the uncut end with picot stitch.

Bead the cut end using fringe, picots, blanket stitch, or whipstitch.

Wear the jabot by draping it around your neck and passing the cut ends through the uncut beaded end (a lark's head knot).

Gallery

MARTHA ARGINSKY
Ellenville, New York

*Mother Nature and the Flower Goddess lariat
with a lampworked bead by Gail Felter Boo
(36"/91.5 cm long).*

BERNIE BRUCE
Saugerties, New York

*Felt swirls pins (5"/12.5 cm and
4 ½/11.5 cm wide), undulating
felt bracelet (11"/28 cm long).*

ELIZABETH BUCHTMAN
Pawling, New York

Two felt scarves (blue 64"/162.5 cm long; orange 49"/124.5 cm long) and one lariat with a lampworked bead by Gail Felter Boo (36"/91.5 cm).

CAROL CYPHER
Esopus, New York

Druzy and felt bead necklace (23"/58.5 cm long), beaded moukaite and felt bead necklace (19"/48.5 cm long).

PHYLLIS DINTENFASS
Appleton, Wisconsin

Felt/glass bead necklace (15"/38 cm long) and lariat (42"/106.5 cm long).

GAIL FELTER BOO
Walden, New York

*Felted flower lariat
(12"/30.5 cm long).*

MARTI HEGQUIST
Farmingdale, New York

Felt bead and glass bead lariat (25¾"/65.5 cm long)

BONNIE HOROWITZ

Fair Lawn, New Jersey
Beaded felt lariat with lampworked bead (16"/40.5 cm long).

MYRNA JARGOWSKY
Ellenville, New York

*Lariat with a lampworked bead by Harold Jargowsky
(20"/51.5 cm long).*

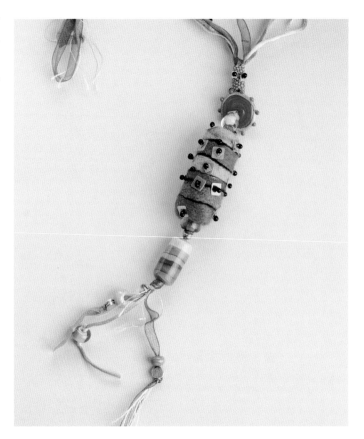

SHELLEY JONES
Richmond, Virginia

*Two necklace cables with beaded felt bead (6"/15 cm diameter), three
pairs of beaded felt earrings (2"/5 cm long), beaded crescent brooch
(2 ¼"/5.5 cm diameter)*

ANNE LUND LORCH
Bolton, Connecticut

Brooch (4½"/11.5 cm long)

BERYL MADDALENA
Nanuet, New York

Felt beads on silver necklace cable (5¾"/14.5 cm diameter).

STEPHANIE MADDALENA
Haverstraw, New York

Felt flower with lampworked bead by Stephanie Maddalena (8"/20.5 cm long).

KAREN OVINGTON
Chicago, Illinois

*Necklace with a lampworked bead by
Karen Ovington (21"/53.5 cm long).*

MAYA RUBINOWITSCH
Oradell, New Jersey

Lariat (32"/81.5 cm long).

CARISSA SCHLESINGER
Marlboro, New Jersey

Felted Day Lily pin (7″/18 cm long).

CAREN SCHWARTZ
Massapequa, New York

Lariat (16″/40.5 cm long).

MONA SELNICK-DOSHAY
Cypress, California

Felted beaded doll pin (7"/18 cm long).

SHERRY SERAFINI
Natrona Heights, Pennsylvania

*Embroidered purse (6" (15 cm) long
without strap, 4½" (11.5 cm) wide;
strap is 22" (56 cm) long) and cuff 6½"
(16.5 cm) long × 3" (7.5 cm) wide.*

Resources

WOOL AND FELTING SUPPLIES

Amazing Threads
www.amazingthreads.com
(845) 336-5322
Wool, felt needles, needles, threads

Carol Cypher
www.carolcypher.com
E-mail: carol@carolcypher.com
Kits, workshops in beadwork/feltmaking, hand-felted jewelry, and personal adornments

Nancy Geisler
woolspinr@taconic.net
Felt needles

The Wool Room
www.woolroom.com
(845) 279-7627
Wool, ingeo, Soy Silk, silk

SEED BEADS AND BEADING SUPPLIES

Beads By Blanche
www.beadsbyblanche.com
(201) 385-6225

Beadzo
(845) 757-5306
Seed, ethnic, vintage, rare and collectible beads

Melek Karacan
(302) 644-3333
Seed beads, lampworked beads

Osiris Beads
www.osirisbeads.com
(231) 933-4853
Seed beads and beading supplies

Sisters' Originals
www.sistersoriginals.com
E-mail: sis@sistersoriginals.com
Marcasite charlottes, seed beads, beaded items

Woodstock Bead Emporium
www.woodstockbeademporium
(845) 679-0066
Seed beads, supplies, Joe Irvin lampworked beads, vintage and Czech beads

LAMPWORKED BEADS

Ellen Black
ehblack@sbcglobal.net
(847) 432-5340

Robert Michael Croft
croft@harbornet.com
(253) 383-2911

Hands of the Hills
www.HOHBead.com
E-mail: HOHBead@aol.com
(206) 232-4588

Harold Jargowsky
beadsinbarn@aol.com

Joe Irvin
www.woodstockbeademporium.com
(845) 679-0066

Olive Glass
Lark Dalton/Corrie Haight
www.oliveglass.com
(360) 468-2821

Nancy Tobey
www.nancytobey.com
E-mail: beads@nancytobey.com
(978) 772-3317

Gail Felter Boo
gboo@hvc.rr.com

Index